AQA

REVISE AQA GCSE

English and English Language

REVISION WORKBOOK

Higher

Series Consultant: Harry Smith

Author: David Grant

THE REVISE AQA SERIES

Available in print or online

Online editions for all titles in the Revise AQA series are available Summer 2013.

Presented on our ActiveLearn platform, you can view the full book and customise it by adding notes, comments and weblinks.

Print editions

English and English Language Revision Workbook Higher
9781447940708

English and English Language Revision Guide Higher
9781447940661

Online editions

English and English Language Revision Workbook Higher
9781447940791

English and English Language Revision Guide Higher
9781447940746

This Revision Workbook is designed to complement your classroom and home learning, and to help prepare you for the exam. It does not include all the content and skills needed for the complete course. It is designed to work in combination with Pearson's main AQA GCSE English 2010 Series.

To find out more visit:
www.pearsonschools.co.uk/aqagcseenglishrevision

ALWAYS LEARNING

PEARSON

Contents

1-to-1 page match with the Revision Guide
ISBN 9781447940661

Section A: Reading

Section B: Writing

A small bit of small print
AQA publishes Sample Assessment Material and the Specification on its website. This is the official content and this book should be used in conjunction with it. The questions in this book have been written to help you practise what you have learned in your revision. Remember: the real exam questions may not look like this.

Questions 1 and 2

The exam paper is split into two sections:

- Section A: Reading
- Section B: Writing

In the Reading section of your exam paper, you will be asked **four** different kinds of question. Each question will ask you to complete one of these types of task:

1 Locate and select relevant information from a source text.

2 Comment on the use of presentation in a source text and its effect on a reader.

3 Identify or infer relevant information from a source text and explain it.

4 Compare the use of language and its effect in two source texts.

Each exam question is intended to assess you on one or both of the assessment objectives:

a *Read and understand texts, selecting material appropriate to purpose.*

b *Explain and evaluate how writers use linguistic, grammatical, structural and presentational features to achieve effects and engage and influence the reader, supporting your comments with detailed textual references.*

Don't try to answer the exam-style questions on this page – just get used to the style.

1 (a) Look at the exam-style question below. For each question, identify the type of task you are being asked to complete and circle either one or both of the assessment objectives on which each question is assessing you.

> **1** What do you learn from **Source 1** about the issues and concerns regarding the farming of genetically modified crops? *(8 marks)*

Task: 1 2 3 4 AOs: **a** **b**

(b)

> **2** Explain how the headline, sub-headline and picture are effective and how they link with the text. *(8 marks)*

Task: 1 2 3 4 AOs: **a** **b**

Questions 3 and 4

In the Reading section of your exam paper, you will be asked **four** different kinds of question. Each question will ask you to complete one of these types of task:

1 Locate and select relevant information from a source text.

2 Comment on the use of presentation in a source text and its effect on a reader.

3 Identify or infer relevant information from a source text and explain it.

4 Compare the use of language and its effect in two source texts.

Each exam question is intended to assess you on one or both of the assessment objectives:

a *Read and understand texts, selecting material appropriate to purpose.*

b *Explain and evaluate how writers use linguistic, grammatical, structural and presentational features to achieve effects and engage and influence the reader, supporting your comments with detailed textual references.*

Don't try to answer the exam-style questions on this page – just get used to the style.

1 Look at the exam-style questions below. For each question, identify the type of task you are being asked to complete and circle either one or both of the assessment objectives on which each question is assessing you.

(a)

3 Now read **Source 3**, *Life and Limb*, which is an extract from a non-fiction book.
Explain some of the thoughts and feelings the writer has as he climbs in the Alps.
(8 marks)

Task: 1 2 3 4 AOs: **a** **b**

(b)

Now you need to refer to **Source 3**, *Life and Limb*, and either **Source 1** or **Source 2**.

4 You are going to compare **two** texts, one of which you have chosen.
Compare the ways in which language is used for effect in the two texts.
Give some examples and analyse what the effects are. *(16 marks)*

Task: 1 2 3 4 AOs: **a** **b**

Planning your exam time

Look at the examples of the kinds of questions you can expect to find in the Reading section of your exam. On the exam paper, you are advised to spend **one hour** on **Section A: Reading** and **one hour** on **Section B: Writing**.

Time allowed
2 hours and 15 minutes

1 What do you learn from **Source 1** about the issues and concerns regarding the farming of genetically modified crops? *(8 marks)*

2 Explain how the headline, sub-headline and picture are effective and how they link with the text. *(8 marks)*

3 Now read **Source 3**, *Life and Limb*, which is an extract from a non-fiction book.
Explain some of the thoughts and feelings the writer has as he climbs in the Alps. *(8 marks)*

Now you need to refer to **Source 3**, *Life and Limb*, and either **Source 1** or **Source 2**.

4 You are going to compare **two** texts, one of which you have chosen.
Compare the ways in which language is used for effect in the two texts.
Give some examples and analyse what the effects are. *(16 marks)*

1 How minutes should you spend reading the source texts and the questions to familiarise yourself with them?

Answer: .... minutes

2 How many minutes should you spend writing your answer to Question 1?

Answer: .... minutes

3 How many minutes should you spend writing your answer to Question 2?

Answer: .... minutes

4 How many minutes should you spend writing your answer to Question 3?

Answer: .... minutes

5 How many minutes should you spend writing your answer to Question 4?

Answer: .... minutes

6 Which of the following should you do before you start to answer any of the questions?
Circle your choices.

Jot down a quick plan of your ideas for each question.	Read the source texts.	Read the questions.	Highlight relevant information to help you answer questions.	Read the source texts a second time.

Had a go ☐ Nearly there ☐ Nailed it! ☐

Reading the questions

Look at the exam-style question below:

> **3** Now read **Source 3**, which is an extract from a non-fiction book. Explain some of the writer's thoughts and feelings as she prepares for her journey to the Arctic. *(8 marks)*

1 Identify:

(a) which source texts you are being asked to write about ....

(b) the keyword in the question which tells you what to do ....

(c) the feature of the texts you are being asked to write about ....

(d) the number of marks for this question ....

(e) how long you should spend writing your answer to this question ....

2 Look at the exam-style questions below. For each question, identify:

- the source text
- the keywords that tell you what to do
- the features you are asked to write about
- the number of marks available
- how long you should spend on each question.

> **1** What do you learn from **Source 1** about the issues and concerns regarding the farming of genetically modified crops? *(8 marks)*
>
> ....

> **2** Explain how the headline, sub-headline and picture in **Source 2** are effective and how they link with the text. *(8 marks)*
>
> ....

> **4** Now you need to refer to **Source 3**, and **either Source 1 or Source 2**. You are going to compare the **two** texts, one of which you have chosen. Compare the different ways in which language is used for effect in the **two** texts. Give some examples and analyse what the effects are. *(16 marks)*
>
> ....

Approaching the exam paper

Before you go into the exam, be sure how you will spend the first 15 minutes of the exam.

Before you start answering the questions, you should be sure you know what they are asking you to do. So look closely at each question in order to:

- identify the source text it is asking you about
- identify the keywords in the question which tell you what to do
- identify the keywords in the question which tell you the feature or features you should write about
- plan how long you will spend answering the question.

Look at the exam-style questions below and then answer Questions 1 and 2 at the bottom of the page.

Section A: Reading

Answer **all** questions in this section.

You are advised to spend about one hour on this section.

Read **Source 1**, the online newspaper article called *If Walls Could Talk* by Kenneth Sugrue.

1 What do you learn from Kenneth Sugrue's article about the pleasures and pitfalls of home improvement? *(8 marks)*

Now read **Source 2**, the article and the picture that goes with it called *How to Tame a Teenager* by Jonathan Gilt.

2 Explain how the headline, sub-headline and picture are effective and how they link to the text. *(8 marks)*

Now read **Source 3**, *In Hannibal's Footsteps*, which is an extract from a non-fiction book.

3 Explain some of the thoughts and feelings the writer has about his experience of travelling over the Alps. *(8 marks)*

Now you need to refer to **Source 3** and **either Source 1 or Source 2**. You are going to compare the **two** texts, one of which you have chosen.

4 Compare the different ways in which language is used for effect in **the two** texts. Give some examples and analyse the effects. *(16 marks)*

1 Circle the key information in all four questions.

2 Use the space below to plan how you would spend the one hour that you should allow for **Section A: Reading**.

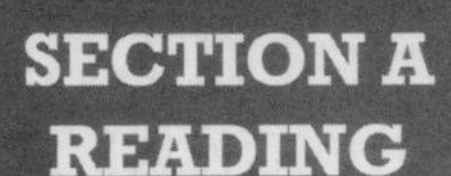

Had a go ☐ Nearly there ☐ Nailed it! ☐

Skimming for the main idea

Look at the headline and opening sentence of the online newspaper article below (**Source 1**), then answer Question 1.

Source 1

Forget meat – there's a world of vegetarian food out there

Climate change is already happening, and we all know we need to make shifts in our personal lifestyle habits to attempt to stem the worst of its effects.

1 What do the headline and the opening sentence suggest the article will be about?

....

....

Now look at the rest of the article below for just 20 seconds, then answer Question 2.

Skim-reading a text can give you a good idea of what it is about before you read it more closely. Look at the headline or title, the first sentence of each paragraph and the last sentence of the text to help you get the main idea of the text.

This week a report from leading water scientists issued one of the sternest warnings yet about global food supplies, saying that the world's population 'may have to switch almost completely to a vegetarian diet over the next 40 years to avoid catastrophic shortages'.

Many of us associate a diet that incorporates meat to be an essential part of a fulfilling life. How do we continue to enjoy our diet when meat is no longer available, or is prohibitively expensive? Well, it might simply require a shift in the way we think about dinnertime.

First, we need to jettison the idea of meat as the centre of the plate, which leads to a search for a 'replacement'. This is what has led us to all those dreadful meat analogues – think about all those dreadful hyper-processed soy patties and fake sausages. So forget all that.

Instead, let us abolish the idea of a 'main dish' and dive into the wonderful world of a meal made up of several smaller dishes that compliment each other. Instead of a giant steak with watery green beans, how about green beans long-simmered in olive oil in the Italian tradition, which renders them silky and rich, topped with quickly sautéed onions and a sprinkle of smoked paprika? This meal can be made in less than an hour, and the leftover beans can become the basis of a bean soup for tomorrow.

Throughout most of our history as eaters, meat has been scarce. This has left us with a rich global legacy of delicious naturally vegetarian dishes. The world itself can be a guide. Vegetarian cooking isn't difficult or pricey. It just asks for a different starting point than we're used to.

2 Sum up the newspaper article in one sentence.

....

....

....

Annotating the sources

Read the opening paragraph of the newspaper article below (**Source 1**), then answer Question 1.

Source 1

How hard it can be to know your child

YOUNG PEOPLE, however good at heart, can enter into a state of being secretive, separate, 'unknowable' to their parents. It's as if, for a while, they walk into a thick mist, an adolescent 'peasouper', and all you can do is wait for them to re-emerge. For parents, this is part waiting game, part grotesque psychological torture: while they are in the mist, anything could happen to their much-loved teenager, young adult ... their child.

1 Which details from **Source 1** would help you to answer the exam-style question below? Tick the ones that are relevant to the question.

3 Explain some of the writer's thoughts and feelings about being a parent. *(8 marks)*

A a thick mist

B all you can do is wait for them to re-emerge

C psychological torture

D much-loved teenager, young adult ... their child

E a state of being secretive

Now look at the rest of the newspaper article, then answer Question 2.

So what do you do? Panic, start refusing to allow your teenager to be 'unknowable'? Start invading their privacy, prying into their Internet activity, clipping every wing you can think of? This is the impulse, the dark side of parental protectiveness. But perhaps to succumb to it would be detrimental to everybody.

Of course I'm not suggesting turning a blind eye. Even the most unknowable, seemingly adult of teenagers, are still essentially (not to mention legally) children. And most are achingly vulnerable and impressionable with it. Nor is there any way of sitting back and watching your own child jump into the fire to see what it feels like to get badly burned.

Perhaps the trick is to take a breath and understand that in the vast majority of cases the unknowable child is probably on the right track. And understand that it might serve us well to stop panicking and try to grasp that, as well as being terrifying, it may be a positive thing. An essential healthy separation. A sign that your child is ready to embrace notions of independence and autonomy. To a place – mentally and emotionally – where they need to be. And, yes, dear panicking, over-protective parents, that does mean without you.

It's true that older children have a tendency to become secretive, mysterious, sometimes even downright underhand. They make really stupid decisions and mistakes – complete howlers. That's why determined, smart parents know they must learn to process this period of child-rearing almost like rolling news, constantly re-adjusting and updating fact and emotions. Then if they're lucky and they keep their nerve, they might just get to see their child walk safely back out of the fog.

2 Highlight any details from the rest of the newspaper article that would help you answer the exam-style question above.

Selecting information

Read the opening paragraph of the newspaper article below (**Source 1**), then answer Question 1.

Source 1

The Skeleton Coast from above

It takes three attempts to shut the cockpit door, and we rock the tiny aircraft in the process. The pilot and trainee, three passengers and too many bags, are all sardined into a tin box on a dusty airstrip, the distant mountains diminished by haze.

1 Which details would help you to answer the exam-style question below? Tick the ones that are relevant to the question.

> **1** What do you learn from the article about where the writer has been and what he has been doing? *(8 marks)*

(a) It takes three attempts to shut the cockpit door

(b) tiny aircraft

(c) The pilot and trainee, three passengers and too many bags

(d) sardined into a tin box

(e) distant mountains

Now look at the rest of the newspaper article, then answer Question 2.

'Clear prop!' The engine splutters into life. Soon we are cantering along, gathering speed and generously throwing up dust for all and sundry. But there is no all, and there is no sundry, just our guide sitting nonchalantly astride the bonnet of his 4×4 to wave off another batch of wilderness seekers. Some distance behind him, two fire buckets hang, lifeless, from a T-shaped frame next to the lavatory, which has a pointed roof made from sticks. That's it. There is no control tower, no emergency services – just miles and miles of nothingness.

We are heading to our camp, a comfortable oasis of calm beside the river. By air it is a relatively straightforward journey; back in the 4×4, it would involve a huge amount of bumping, churning and sliding over desert rock and sand to get there.

The altimeter needle continues to turn as the views widen; detail is lost as patterns emerge, nature's patterns, completely devoid of influence from man's busying hand. At cruising height, the desert gives way to mountains, carved and fissured rock massifs.

Dry rivers trace steep-sided valleys, where twin lines of hardy bushes mark the boundaries of an infrequent flow of water. But within this seeming barrenness is life.

We have witnessed the regal oryx with his lethal horns, striding the plains and scampering up mountain slopes; the desert-adapted rhino with his grumpy ways, his lumbering, trundling gait. The list goes on; life goes on, resilient, changing.

Then the pilot smiles and offers us a spherical bag. 'We're landing soon to refuel – anyone for biltong?'

2 Highlight any information from the rest of the article that would help you answer the exam-style question above.

Purpose and audience

Look at the different texts below. For each one, identify the writer's intended audience and purpose. For each of your answers, write a sentence explaining your decision.

The first things you should think about when you have read a text are its purpose and its audience. Note, though, you won't be asked **directly** in the exam to identify a text's purpose and audience.

Guided

1 Kanye Omari West was born in 1977. His father was a former activist and photographer, his mother a university English professor. With four Number 1 albums under his belt, West diversified, launching a fashion range and a chain of fast food restaurants, all of which have contributed to the huge amount of money donated to his charitable foundation supporting African American children's education.

The audience for this text is teenagers and younger adults because I think they would be interested in Kanye West, although the formal language makes it appropriate for all adults.

The purpose of the text is to ....

....

....

....

2 Eating a healthy dinner at school could make the biggest difference to your education. It can help your concentration and, when you're concentrating, you learn more. It's not just about how much you eat – it's what you eat that really matters. And don't think it's just 'lay off the chips and chocolate'. You need fruit and vegetables as well – five portions of them everyday.

....

....

....

....

3 Sitting in our cabin, staring out at the snow, we witnessed one of the most extraordinary sights of our lives. As we watched, a herd of reindeer approached. The first thing that strikes you about them is their size. They're enormous. And despite their huge heads and ungainly antlers, they are astonishingly beautiful. Even the bald one with huge clumps of matted fur dangling from its backside like Christmas decorations.

....

....

....

....

Had a go ☐ Nearly there ☐ Nailed it! ☐

Putting it into practice

Read **Source 1** below, then have a go at the exam-style question opposite.

Source 1

GET USED TO 'EXTREME' WEATHER, IT'S THE NEW NORMAL

Climate change and weather extremes are not about a distant future. Formerly one-off extreme weather episodes seem to be becoming the new normal. Weather extremes are not that extreme any more. Heatwaves, floods, droughts and wildfires are the new reality of an ever warming world.

And this should not come as a surprise. Scientists have been warning for years that as the planet heats up, we will have to deal with more severe, more changeable, more unpredictable weather. The evidence is mounting that human-caused warming is pushing normal warming effects to extremes. Heatwaves have increased in duration and frequency. Some parts of Europe are now gripped by severe water shortages while other parts have suffered extreme precipitations causing floods and increased crop losses.

And although not every extreme weather event can be attributed to climate change, scientists are now much more confident about linking individual weather events to climate change. Take 2011's record warm November in the UK, the second hottest on record. Researchers say that it was at least 60 times more likely to happen because of climate change than because of natural variations in the earth's weather systems.

Global climate breakdown is occurring more rapidly than most climate scientists had expected. Climate change is happening, and it exacerbates a whole range of other global problems, adding further instability in an already unstable world.

But isn't it too costly to invest in a low-carbon world, some may ask? Well, yes it costs. But so does business-as-usual. It would be wrong to believe that to continue business-as-usual is the cheap option. It is not. On the contrary, it is very expensive.

Businesses don't need to be told about the financial losses caused by weather extremes. This summer's drought in the US devastated the multibillion-dollar corn and soybean crops. Insurers in the USA may face as much as $20bn losses this year, their biggest ever loss in agriculture. This is not exactly helping fight the economic crisis.

It is simply incredible what big risks some people are prepared to take on behalf of future generations. Despite the facts and evidence in front of us, there are still many interests advocating doing nothing or continuing with business-as-usual. Or just forgetting the climate crisis until we have solved the economic crisis.

And whereas some see the current financial turmoil as a bitter setback for international climate protection, I see intelligent climate action as a driver of new opportunities for jobs in Europe, for investments in energy efficiency technologies, for boosting innovation and competitiveness, for lowering energy bills.

To me, tackling the climate crisis helps, not damages, our economic security and prosperity. Both crises are interlinked and must be tackled together.

Putting it into practice

1 What do you learn from **Source 1** about the effects of climate change? *(8 marks)*

When you tackle this kind of question in the exam, remember to:

- spend around 10–15 minutes answering it
- read the source text carefully, highlighting any information about the effects of climate change
- select key points that are relevant to the question
- avoid copying out chunks of text.

Remember: You will have more space than this to answer the question in the exam. Use your own paper to finish your answer to the question above.

Had a go ☐ Nearly there ☐ Nailed it! ☐

The writer's viewpoint

Read the headline and the opening of the newspaper article below (**Source 1**), then answer Question 1.

Source 1

We have become a nation of cry-babies!

Ah, such wonderful news that Europe won the Ryder Cup! We beat America, we trounced the Yankee's doodle dandy, we snatched victory from almost certain defeat, making this golf tournament the final magnificent huzzah in a long summer of sporting glory which ... hang on a minute. Why are all these men in blue plaid jackets and neat slacks standing around, crying fit to burst? Why are they weeping like bridesmaids who've just had their bouquets nicked? Buck up, Ryder team.

1 Write one or two sentences summing up the writer's viewpoint.

....

....

....

....

....

....

....

Now read more of the article, then answer Questions 2 and 3.

There is a worrying side to all this. Yes, crying can be good for emotional health, but what happens when the rough stuff of life hits you square in the jaw?

Your prospects of coping with a genuine dilemma or emergency are slim to nil.

Surely there is a need to conserve emotions; to store tears for the times that really matter, for the great trials of life that lie ahead, as surely they must.

Far too many people cry for no other reason than they are feeling sorry for themselves.

Get a grip. On your hankie, if nothing else.

2 Do you still think your answer to Question 1 effectively sums up the writer's viewpoint? If not, write another sentence or two, summing up their viewpoint.

....

....

....

....

3 Write down three short quotations from the article that helped you to answer Questions 1 and 2, then write one or two sentences explaining how each one helped you to work out the writer's viewpoint.

(a) ....

....

....

(b) ....

....

....

(c) ....

....

....

A short quotation could even be a one-word quotation. Sometimes the writer's language choice can tell you a lot about their viewpoint.

Fact, opinion and expert evidence

Look at the three extracts from online articles below, then answer Question 1.

A Last year, more than 800 businesses failed each and every day.

B Professor Trevor Carter's research strongly suggests that poverty is the root cause.

C There is nothing more delicious than warm, fresh bread.

1 Identify which of these extracts is:

(a) a fact ....   **(b)** an opinion ....   **(c)** expert evidence ....

Now read the newspaper article (**Source 1**) below, and answer Questions 2 and 3.

Source 1

How GM crops have increased the use of danger pesticides and created superweeds and toxin-resistant insects

Planting GM crops has led to an increase rather than a decrease in the use of pesticides in the last 16 years, according to US scientists. The researchers said that the plants have caused superweeds and toxin-resistant insects to emerge, meaning farmers not only have to use more pesticides on their crops overall, but also are using older and more dangerous chemicals. The team at Washington State University found the weight of chemicals used on US farms has increased by 183 million kilos since GM crops were introduced in 1996.

The findings dramatically undermine the case for adopting the crops, which were sold to farmers and shoppers on the basis that they would reduce the need to be treated with powerful chemicals. However, the reality is that a number of weeds have developed an immunity to the chemical and are now able to swamp farmers' fields. The overall effect is that desperate farmers are now using a cocktail of many different chemicals to try and tame the weeds.

Study leader Professor Charles Benbrook said: 'Resistant weeds have become a major problem for many farmers reliant on GM crops and are now driving up the volume of herbicide needed each year by about 25 per cent.'

2 Write one sentence summing up the writer's viewpoint in the article.

....

....

3 Identify at least one fact, one opinion and one piece of expert evidence the writer has used to support his viewpoint, then write a sentence explaining how it does this.

Fact: ....

....

Opinion: ....

....

Expert evidence: ....

....

Had a go ☐ Nearly there ☐ Nailed it! ☐

Inference

Read the opening of a newspaper article about foxes, then answer Questions 1 and 2.

> They are as big as Alsatians and getting bigger. Their numbers are increasing and are out of control. They foul our gardens, they rip cats apart. It is simply a matter of time before they kill a baby.

1 Write down two words or phrases from the article which suggest we should be worried about foxes.

(a) ....

(b) ....

Guided **2** What impression of foxes does the article give you?

The article makes me think that foxes are ....

....

Now read the rest of the article, then answer Question 3.

> It's incredible how much hysteria the British press can generate about such a small, and largely inoffensive, animal as the fox.
>
> In the war on the urban fox, truth is irrelevant. The fox "cub" recently pictured sitting on a child's bed in London was actually an adult in the terminal stages of mange. It had crept into the house to try to keep warm (foxes with mange lose most of their fur): it caused no problem and was removed by the RSPCA. A non-story and an everyday occurrence with stray cats.
>
> The first claim that foxes will kill a baby appeared in the Sunday Times in 1973: 40 years on, this still has not happened. In comparison, the seven children and five adults killed by dogs since 2005, and the hundreds more disfigured, receive far less coverage.

Guided **3** Explain some of the writer's thoughts and feelings about urban foxes. Remember to use at least one short quotation from the text to support your answer.

> Use inference to work out the writer's attitude – and don't be misled by the use of sarcasm or by other opinions which the writer includes then dismisses.

The writer begins the article by making foxes sound aggressive and dangerous. He describes the fox population as 'out of control' and describing how they can 'rip cats apart'. This horrific picture shocks the reader, but it then seems that the writer is mocking this as examples of the 'hysteria' with which the British press presents urban foxes.

As the article goes on, the writer develops his point. He ....

....

....

....

....

....

Point-Evidence-Explain

Read the newspaper article below (**Source 1**), then answer the questions that follow.

Source 1

Coping with the first day at school

For some youngsters, walking through those school gates in their uniform for the first time provokes great excitement. Others find it thoroughly nerve-wracking as they enter the great unknown.

Every child is different – and as the mother of three daughters I should know. My eldest girl couldn't have been more thrilled about the prospect of sitting in a classroom and we counted down the days for weeks beforehand. In the event she thought it was all a huge let-down and ended her first day adamant that it would be her last. When we explained that she had many years of schooling ahead of her she was livid.

An effective way to support your answers to questions that ask you to explain or compare is to use Point-Evidence-Explain paragraphs.

1 The point below could be used to comment on the writer's use of language and its effect. Which piece of evidence from **Source 1** most effectively supports it?

Point: The writer uses contrasting language to emphasise how differently children can react to their first day at school.

Evidence A: 'nerve-wracking', 'great excitement'

Evidence B: 'Every child is different'

To develop your point and evidence, you need to explain how they answer the question.

....

....

2 Which of these explanations most effectively develops the point and the supporting evidence?

Point:
Evidence

The writer uses contrasting language to emphasise how differently children can react to their first day at school. For example, she compares a child who finds the experience 'nerve-wracking' and one who regards it with 'great excitement'.

Explain A: These two very different language choices emphasise and exaggerate how differently children can react.

Explain B: The writer has chosen to highlight two extreme and opposite reactions using emotive language. This emphasises the strength of children's feelings when they first go to school and how difficult this can be for parents.

3 Write one or two sentences, explaining which explanation you think is more effective and why.

....

....

Had a go ☐ Nearly there ☐ Nailed it! ☐

Putting it into practice

Read **Source 1** below, then have a go at the exam-style question opposite.

Source 1

Sir Ranulph Fiennes: it's the winning that is important

At the age of 68, most men are collecting their bus pass. But not 'the world's greatest explorer', who is shuffling around a large warehouse near Bedford, desperately searching for his mobile telephone.

Sir Ranulph Fiennes – the only man to circumnavigate the globe on foot, traversing through both poles; conquer Everest, after suffering a heart attack on a previous attempt; climb the north face of the Eiger, despite suffering vertigo so badly that it is his wife who has to clean the gutters at home; and run seven marathons in seven days on seven continents for good measure – is on another mission.

First, though, he needs to find his phone amid the morass of polar equipment laid out on the floor. Having located it, he mutters and peers suspiciously at the screen before an aide explains that he has 43 voicemail messages. Ran, as he likes to be called, looks at me: 'I have no idea how this thing works.' I'm worried that his latest expedition might be a step too far if mastering a simple old Nokia is beyond him.

In December, as part of a six-man team, he will set off to cross the bleak wasteland of Antarctica – a task that has been achieved before, but never in the depths of midwinter, when the temperature averages –70C and occasionally plummets to –90C. The expedition has been nicknamed 'The Coldest Journey'.

I have joined him at an engineering centre in Bedford to see how the equipment fares at ultra low temperatures. In the warehouse is a glorified walk-in freezer. The electronic gauge on the outside wall reads –58.7C. I am given a pair of salopettes, boots and an ultra-thick down jacket.

At first, my body feels toasty warm, and apart from my nostrils icing up, I am fairly comfortable. Except for my hands. After five minutes, they go from a little cold to 'Um, actually, Ran, my fingers are in quite a bit of pain.'

He ignores me. I am not sure whether this is because his hearing is starting to go – he often cocks his head and says 'Eh?' – or because he thinks I am a wimp. Here, after all, is a man who has such a disregard for pain that he hacked off his own frostbitten fingers. He did this not in last-resort desperation on an expedition, but calmly in his garden shed because he did not fancy the idea of waiting five months for an operation. 'My wife said I was becoming very irritable every time I knocked them, so I bought a micro sword in the village shop.' He clamped his hand in a Black & Decker vice and proceeded to hack away. For five whole days. 'It didn't hurt at all. The surgeon at the hospital said I had done a very good job.' The top third of all of the fingers and thumb on his left hand are now stumps.

After 11 minutes in the cold chamber, I panic amid visions of my frozen hand requiring the Black & Decker treatment. 'I really need to leave now, I'm sorry,' I say in as forceful a way as possible for someone feeling very sheepish.

Putting it into practice

1 What do you learn about Ranulph Fiennes from the article? *(8 marks)*

When you tackle this kind of question in the exam, remember to:

- spend around 10–15 minutes answering it
- read the source text carefully, highlighting any information about Ranulph Fiennes
- select key points that are relevant to the question
- avoid copying out chunks of text.

Remember: You will have more space than this to answer the question in the exam. Use your own paper to finish your answer to the question above.

Had a go ☐ Nearly there ☐ Nailed it! ☐

Identifying presentational devices 1

Look at the webpage below.

1 Look at the labels around the webpage. Draw a line from each one to an example of that presentational feature on the webpage.

2 Underneath each label, write one or two sentences commenting on:

(a) the effect of the feature on the reader

(b) how it helps the text achieve its purpose and get the writer's viewpoint across.

Fonts

....

....

....

....

....

Headings

....

....

....

....

....

Putting your child first.
Visiting our hospital

Orchard Place Hospital for Children

Hospital | Charity

Patients | Parents | Staff | News | Vacancies

Your visit | Your care | Your life

Do your bit!
Orchard Place Hospital Charity

Find more information
search

Colour

....

....

....

....

....

....

Images

....

....

....

....

....

....

Logo/Do your bit!

....

....

....

....

....

....

Identifying presentational devices 2

Look at the webpage below.

1 Look at the labels around the webpage below. Draw a line from each one to an example of that structural feature on the webpage.

2 Underneath each label, write one or two sentences commenting on:

(a) the effect of the feature on the reader

(b) how it helps the text achieve its purpose and get the writer's viewpoint across.

News | Weather | Sport | Politics | Search

UK footballers paid 1,500% more than 20 years ago

Footballers have seen their wages rise by over 1,500% over the past 20 years, compared to the 186% increase in the average UK wages, according to a new study.
Research from the High Pay Centre shows that top players have seen bumper pay rises, while those playing for lower division have seen their pay rise by significantly less.

The High Pay Centre research also revealed the impact of these wages on fans, saying they are the ones 'paying the price' of excessive pay:

- the lowest ticket available has increased by over 1,000% since 1989
- the cheapest ticket to watch Liverpool has increased from £4 to £45
- English clubs account for approximately 56% of all debt in top flight clubs across Europe – despite only representing 2% of clubs
- over half of English football league clubs have been insolvent in the past 20 years.

Premier League Wage Bills 2010–2011	
Chelsea	£191 million
Manchester City	£174 million
Liverpool	£135 million
Arsenal	£124 million

Nick Isles, Chair of the High Pay Centre said the figures show it is 'time to put the brakes on this dramatic escalation in pay at the top'.

Bullet points

The writer has used bullet points to ....

Tables ....

Sections/boxes ....

Paragraphs ....

Had a go ☐ Nearly there ☐ Nailed it! ☐

Using P-E-E to comment on presentational devices

Look carefully at the presentational and structural features of the newspaper article below (**Source 1**), then answer the questions that follow.

Source 1

The dogs who listen to children reading

Scheme aims to encourage children to read aloud

When children read to him, Danny does not criticise or correct their pronunciation. He just nods and pricks up an ear, although sometimes he closes his eyes and appears not to be listening.

Danny is a dog and a novel way of encouraging pupils at Oakhill primary school in Tamworth, Staffordshire, to read aloud.

Some children show the dog the pictures as they read.

1 Look at these six extracts from one student's comments on presentation. Organise them into two Point-Evidence-Explanation paragraphs.

A Although it is a clear statement literally summarising the content of the article, the connection it makes between 'dogs', 'listen' and 'reading' is surprising, amusing and intriguing.

B Together the headline and the subheading summarise the article and, to an extent, spoil the surprise that the writer has tried to create in the opening paragraph of the article: the reader has already guessed that Danny is a dog before the writer reveals it.

C The subheading adds further information to the headline.

D The headline attracts the reader's attention, not only because it is in a large, bold font, but also because of its choice of language.

E It explains the intentions of the scheme to 'encourage' reading aloud.

F The writer uses this surprising summary to capture the reader's interest, encouraging them to read the article and discover more. It also suggests the humorous tone with which the article will treat this subject.

Remember: You not only need to **explain** how the headline, the subheading or the picture are effective, you also need to **comment** on how they link with the text, thinking about how they help the text to achieve its purpose and get the writer's viewpoint across.

2 Write a Point-Evidence-Explanation paragraph explaining how the image in **Source 1** is effective and how it links with the text.

....

....

....

....

Commenting on headlines

Look at the headlines below.

A

How do I look? Electrifying!

Fancy dress shocker ends in hospital

A man dressed as a Christmas tree got more of a shock than he bargained for when he tried switching on the Christmas lights he had used to decorate his costume.

B

Success story

Self-published ebook hits the bestseller list

A LANCASHIRE HOUSEWIFE has become one of the most successful ebook authors of all time.

C

Tiny ideas for tiny minds

Politicians are constantly underestimating voters' intelligence

Politicians' desperate attempts to communicate with voters are frequently based on an assumption that most of us are complete idiots.

D

Would you trust a politician?

Survey shows public trust in our MPs at an all time low

1 Which headlines have withheld information? ....

2 Which headlines use alliteration? ....

3 Which headlines use repetition? ....

4 Which headlines use a rhetorical question? ....

5 Which headlines reflect the tone of the article that follows? ....

6 Which subheadings add more detail to the story? ....

Guided 7 Choose two of the headlines above. Write one or two sentences about each one, commenting on:

(a) any significant features **(b)** their effect on the reader **(c)** how they link with the text.

Headline .... uses ....

....

The effect of this is ....

....

....

....

....

Had a go ☐ Nearly there ☐ Nailed it! ☐

Image and effect

Read the headline and opening sentence of the newspaper article below (**Source 1**), then answer the questions.

Source 1

School dinners: still not pulling in the punters

Despite numerous campaigns, policies and celebrity appeals, a significant number of school canteens are still failing to attract their target audience: school kids. Fed at home on a diet of nuggets and chips, is it any wonder that kids' eyes aren't lighting up at the sight of school broccoli?

1 Which image would you choose to illustrate this article? (Circle **A**, **B**, **C** or **D**.)

A

B

C

D

Write one or two sentences explaining your choice of image. Aim to comment on:

- why you feel the image supports the point of view expressed in the newspaper article
- the effect you hope the image will have on the reader.

....

....

....

....

....

....

....

....

Linking comments on presentation to the text

Look at the headline and text below (**Source 1**), then answer Question 1.

Source 1

Cherish the grey army of volunteers – none of us would survive without their dedication

WITHIN THE NEXT 10 YEARS, the global population of oldsters (defined by the United Nations as over-60s) will reach one billion. There are already more over-60s than under-fives on the planet.

And this is surely good news. Yes, over-60s have fewer years of working and paying taxes ahead of them than under-fives. But on the plus side, they rarely scream, they are almost never covered in chocolate spread, and they are much more likely to give you a sweet than demand one.

I have just returned home from a weekend at Wigtown Book Festival. Without the volunteer power of the over-60s all year round, I'm not sure any book festival would happen.

1 Look at these words from the headline. Answer the questions about them, focusing on the writer's language choices and their effect on the reader.

Cherish This is an imperative or command. It tells the reader what to do. What effect does the writer intend?

....

....

army What does this word suggest about elderly volunteers?

....

....

none of us Why does the writer choose the word 'us'? Why 'none', not 'some'?

....

....

survive What effect does this emotive language choice have on the reader?

....

....

2 How does the effect of this headline link with the effect of the text? Write a paragraph explaining your ideas.

....

....

....

....

....

Remember: Headlines and other presentational features can help the text appeal to its audience, achieve its purpose, and reinforce its viewpoint.

Had a go ☐ Nearly there ☐ Nailed it! ☐

Selecting evidence

Victoria Pendleton is an Olympic gold medal winning cyclist. Read **Source 1**, which is a short extract from her autobiography entitled *Between the Lines*, then answer Questions 1 and 2.

> Dad rode away from me as we climbed the hill on a cold and drizzly Sunday morning in Bedfordshire. 'He doesn't love me,' I said to myself as I tried to keep up with the distant figure of my father. 'He doesn't love me. He doesn't love me …'
>
> I repeated the words over and over again as, never lifting my gaze from the unbreakable man on the bike climbing the steep hill, I turned my legs as fast as I could. I had to hang onto Dad. I was sure that if I lost sight of him I would lose hold of his love.

1 Which of the quotes below would you use in an answer to this question:

> **3** Explain some of Victoria Pendleton's thoughts and feelings as she trains with her father. *(8 marks)*

A cold and drizzly Sunday morning

B 'He doesn't love me. He doesn't love me …'

C unbreakable

D the distant figure of my father

E if I lost sight of him I would lose hold of his love.

2 Choose **two** quotations that you think will allow you to comment on the writer's choice of language. Write one or two sentences about each one, commenting on its effect and what it tells you about Victoria Pendleton's thoughts and feelings.

> Make sure you choose quotations that:
> - allow you to focus on answering the question
> - contain a word, phrase or sentence structure that you think the writer has used for effect.

Quote 1:...

....

....

Quote 2:...

....

....

Now read the next paragraphs from Pendleton's autobiography, then answer Question 3.

> I was fifteen. I had grown used to the ritual of chasing my father as he sped ahead of me. Dad dealt in clear and simple truths. He never told you that you were better than you were – even to boost you at your most vulnerable. Dad just expected you to do your best every single day. He was tough but, when I pleased him, I felt radiant with happiness. I knew how much it meant when Dad said he was proud of me.
>
> The rain trickled down my face. It might have looked like I was crying, but I wasn't. I was just concentrating and pedalling, pedalling and concentrating. But I was so tired and freezing I would no longer feel my hands on the handlebars or my feet on the pedals. I held on, numb to the finger-tips, pushing down with my churning legs and deadened feet. The gap between us might have widened but I would not let myself lose Dad. I clung onto the blurry image of him up ahead. An invisible twine must have bound his bike to mine.

3 Underline at least two more quotations that you could include in an answer to the exam-style question above.

Embedding quotations

Read the opening of the newspaper article below (**Source 1**), then answer Question 1.

Source 1

My message to the parents who can't let their children go: grow up

Modern parenting seems to be in trouble when it comes to managing the boundaries between the generations. In some households, Mum and Dad pretend to be their children's 'best friends'. They may even become fans of the same boy bands or share a tent at Glastonbury. They splash cash and offer 24-hour catering. It's even rumoured that – if begged – they'll do homework or pass their child's exams. All of which indicates to me there's a crisis in Parentland.

1 Using the short quotations shown in **A–E**, explain the writer's point of view.

A pretend

B 'best friends'

C share a tent at Glastonbury

D splash cash

E crisis

The writer feels that there is a 'crisis' in parenting as parents seem to want to be their children's 'best friends'. This includes such extremes as parents who ....

....

Worse still, the writer suggests that parents only 'pretend' to be their childrens' friend which suggests that ....

....

Now read more of the article, then answer Question 2.

Consider the case of the black-headed gull – a pest in some eyes – but probably a better parent than we humans. Mother bird simply locks the larder once junior can fly, having attained an adult size and weight. The rule is simple: 'No more regurgitated mackerel for you, my pet, find your own!' Days will pass while outraged child prods her with the cry of 'Gimme' like some stroppy teenager deprived of broadband. But the young bird adapts. It has to. The law of our animal kingdom says there's a time to grow up. A time that we as social animals sometimes seem determined to push into middle age.

2 Write one sentence explaining what you learn from the extract about the writer's thoughts and feelings regarding parenting.

....

3 Circle four or five short quotations that you could use to support your answer to Question 2.

4 Rewrite your answer to Question 2 embedding at least two of the quotations you have circled.

....

....

Remember: Shorter quotations are often more effective than longer ones.

- They show that you can identify key words and phrases in the text.
- They allow you to focus on the writer's specific language choices.
- You don't waste time and ink copying out large chunks of the source text.

Had a go ☐ Nearly there ☐ Nailed it! ☐

Putting it into practice

Read **Source 1** below, then have a go at the exam-style question opposite.

Source 1

THE NEW GLOBAL ADDICTION: SMARTPHONES

We're becoming addicted to iPhones and BlackBerrys – and it's not only manners that suffer.

Damian Thompson

Who would have thought, 20 years ago, that a plastic and glass box smaller than the palm of your hand would ruin the good manners of millions of people?

Yes, we know about the digital miracles wrought by the smartphone. But there's no more powerful measure of its growing influence on our lives than the sudden shattering – in less than a decade – of standards of etiquette dating back centuries.

Imagine two 1950s housewives meeting for tea and pastries in a department store. One of them is chirping about some teak dining room chairs that she thinks her husband will adore. But the other woman, instead of nodding politely, fishes her engagement diary out of her handbag and flicks through its pages with glazed eyes. That would be the last time those ladies met for tea, I fancy.

These days, in contrast, many of Britain's 30 million smartphone owners think nothing of surreptitiously checking Twitter during a conversation. Usually this digital rudeness takes place while someone else is talking: a spouse, friend, colleague or boss. But younger smartphone users have mastered the art of texting one person while talking to another. You need only travel on the top of a London bus to see virtuoso demonstrations of this trick by teenagers.

Turned off: many of Britain's 30 million smartphone owners think nothing of checking Twitter during a conversation. (Photo: *Getty Images*)

Putting it into practice

2 Explain how the headline, subheading and picture are effective and how they link to the text. *(8 marks)*

When you tackle this kind of question in the exam, remember to:

- spend around 10–15 minutes answering it
- make specific comments about language choice
- comment on the effect of each feature on the reader
- comment on how the effect is created
- comment on how these features link to the text by helping it achieve its purpose and reinforce its viewpoint.

Remember: You will have more space than this to answer the question in the exam. Use your own paper to finish your answer to the question above.

Had a go ☐ Nearly there ☐ Nailed it! ☐

Develop your explanations

Read the opening of the newspaper article below (**Source 1**).

Source 1

I was crushed by a cow

I look after about 300 cows on a farm in Gloucestershire and have built up a natural affinity with them – but I still remain wary. Three years ago, I was moving the Friesian herd out of a field and one rather lame cow crept up silently behind me. I waved my hands at her and shouted, 'Get back!' I wasn't concerned, just slightly irritated that she'd followed me. But as I turned to walk back to the yard, a force like the bonnet of a fast-moving car exploded in my back, throwing me facedown on the concrete track. It's not unusual for a cow to follow someone, but I'd never had a solitary beast charge at me like that.

Look at some extracts from one student's comments on the writer's thoughts and feelings, then complete the questions below.

A The writer knows a lot about cows because he says he looks after 'about 300' of them.

B The writer emphasises the impact of the cow by describing it as a 'force' which he compares to a 'fast-moving car' that 'exploded in my back'.

C The word 'exploded' suggests the impact of the cow was extremely sudden, shocking and violent.

D After the incident, the writer describes the cow as a 'beast', which reinforces the impression that it is an unpredictable and dangerous animal. This contrasts sharply with the initial description of the cow as 'rather lame' and the fact that the writer 'wasn't concerned', making the incident all the more shocking and violent.

E The writer says he was thrown 'facedown on the concrete track', which must have been painful.

1 Circle any relevant and effective comments on the writer's thoughts and feelings above.

2 What would be the best order for your chosen comments? List them in order.

....

3 Now read another short extract from the article. Write two or three relevant and effective comments on the writer's thoughts and feelings.

Shocked and winded, I rolled over and tried to get up, but the cow lowered her head and pushed it into my chest and stomach, crushing me into the ground. I felt the back legs of the 1,000lb beast folding, and realised she was going to sit on me.

It's hard to comprehend just how big a cow is until you're underneath one, looking up at it. I've no idea what made her so angry – I've waved at cows before and they've always backed off. But this one seemed possessed.

....

....

....

Word classes

Read the opening of the newspaper article below (**Source 1**), then answer Questions 1 and 2.

Source 1

At a loss in the Rocky Mountains

I lose handbags; I leave them behind when travelling – Italy (on a train), Norway (in a mountain cabin), Scotland (in a distillery). I had a safe canvas bag with a shoulder strap for Canada.

We headed along Highway One, the Trans-Canada Highway, a straight line far into the distance.

'You'd think the Romans had been here,' my husband said.

Not the Romans but the early pioneers, enterprising adventurers going west, not knowing what lay ahead. We knew. We were going to the Rocky Mountains. The land was flat as we left Calgary, the sprawling development making it difficult to know exactly when we did leave. Then we saw the profiles of the ski jumps, challenging monsters for other brave men, a legacy from the Winter Olympic Games in 1988. We stopped to take photographs and decided to have lunch in a local café.

1 Circle and label at least one noun, one verb, one adjective and one adverb in the extract.

2 In the opening sentence, the writer has used lots of **proper nouns:** Italy, Norway, Scotland.

What effect does this list of proper nouns create?

....

....

....

Read more of the article, then answer Questions 3 and 4.

Then on again, the road developing ups and downs as the hills became mountains. We drove slowly, taking in the ever more spectacular view. At times it felt that we were diving down into a bowl surrounded by peaks. Just scribbles of cloud in the blue sky, the mountain tops clear, inviting photos that would never do justice to the landscape. When we reached Canmore, a ski resort near Banff, we decided to stop for a look around and to imagine the place in winter.

I opened the car door and reached down by my feet for my handbag. Not there. Nor on the back seat. I stood immobile as I relived the last hour or so of my life. The picture was as clear as that of the ski jumps. It was on the floor by my chair in the café.

3 Choose **one verb** from the extract above that you think is particularly effective. Write a sentence explaining the effect this verb has on the reader.

....

....

4 Find one or two sentences in the extract in which the writer has used lots of adjectives. What effect do they create?

....

....

....

....

....

....

Had a go ☐ Nearly there ☐ Nailed it! ☐

Putting it into practice

Read **Source 1** below, then have a go at the exam-style question opposite.

Source 1

Experience: I lost the power of language

That morning, I got the train as always. I was a publishing director and was looking forward to reading my newspaper, as usual. I would always turn to the cryptic crossword, but that day it didn't make any sense. I'd been doing it for 30-odd years, but trying to read this one was like treading through treacle: incredibly slow and hard. I thought I must be tired.

At the office, I sat down, turned on my computer and found I couldn't read the message on the screen. I said to my assistant, 'This is strange, I can't make my computer work', and she started laughing. Although I had no idea at the time, I was speaking gibberish.

Eventually, worried colleagues contacted my wife, Beth, and she drove me straight to hospital. There, confirmation came that I'd had a stroke in the part of my brain that deals with communication. I was now suffering from aphasia, a condition that means it's difficult or impossible to receive and produce language. When Beth asked the consultant how long it would take for me to get better, he replied, 'How long is a piece of string?'

Over that first day, I got progressively worse. I couldn't understand what people were saying; I couldn't speak intelligibly; I couldn't read or write. A couple of nights later, I had to go to the loo and realised I couldn't read the signs on the doors. That was the first time I thought, 'This is serious.' It was the only time I cried.

I was back at home a week later, and my goal was to get better and return to work in a couple of months. I started seeing a speech therapist three times a week, and was given homework to help rebuild my vocabulary and grammar. I'd look at simple pictures and try to describe them as my mind wandered round and round in the darkness, looking for words.

Apart from being incredibly tired, and sleeping for hours and hours, I felt healthy. But I was deeply confused. Sitting around the table with my wife and children, all I could hear was a babble of noise. I couldn't separate sounds, be it a dog barking outside, music in the background or my wife talking to me. It was hugely frustrating. After a month, my own speech became functional – 'Could you pass the salt?' 'Shall we go for a walk?' – but I couldn't have a conversation. I couldn't read the newspaper. When I sat down to my favourite television programme, The Sopranos, I couldn't understand a thing. I felt isolated.

My speech came back, and I learned how to read again, albeit much more slowly. I also learned patience, and the ability to zone out of conversations when I couldn't keep up. I spent more time outside, looking after our garden, and eventually got a job a couple of days a week at a nursery. I allowed myself to slow down, and started to enjoy it.

Gradually, I sloughed off my old skin. I grieved the past, its passing and its absence, and started to come to terms with it. Now, 10 years later, I look after my grandson one day a week, and my relationship with my family is deeper than ever. We have learned to be very patient with each other. I'm no longer a high-achieving publisher or someone who reads 10 books a week. I'm a family man and gardener with aphasia, and if I read 10 books a year, that's pretty good.

Putting it into practice

3 Explain some of the writer's thoughts and feelings as he comes to terms with his medical condition. *(8 marks)*

When you tackle this kind of question in the exam, remember to:
- spend around 10–15 minutes answering it
- read the source text carefully, highlighting any clues about the writer's thoughts and feelings
- support all your points with evidence and a clear explanation focusing on **effect**.

Remember: You will have more space than this to answer the question in the exam. Use your own paper to finish your answer to the question above.

Connotations

Read the opening of the newspaper article below (**Source 1**), then answer Question 1.

Source 1

Treat it well and telly will be a faithful family friend

One major difference between my childhood home and the more sober dwellings of many peers was that the TV was barely ever switched off. If Dad wasn't watching the racing, my mother would be catching the news. My sharp-elbowed brothers would channel-hop for football, while my big sister and I loved Hollywood weepies.

Despite our small-screen dependency, my siblings and I devoured books and roamed outside.

1 **(a)** Which ideas and attitudes might the two circled words from the text suggest to the reader?

....

....

....

(b) Draw a line between the circled words and their possible connotations.

dependency devoured

addiction large quantity drugs reliance choice

2 Write down any other connotations that you think either of the highlighted words has.

....

....

....

....

Connotations are the ideas or attitudes that a word or phrase suggests to the reader.

Read more of the article, then answer Question 3.

Now, while I share concerns about the addictive and stultifying qualities of many computer games, I am not so convinced of the evils of the goggle-box. Let me qualify that statement by adding I would rather put a fork through my hand than allow my two boys a TV in their bedroom, but that's because, in so doing, you change the status of television from slave to master.

You also declare 'TV Rules, OK?' when you install a screen so vast that it towers over your living room like an alien invader from Planet Currys. If, however, you have one modest-sized set in a house full of books, pens, CDs and Lego, then I doubt your offspring's brains will atrophy just because they watched CBeebies. The few facts my boys hold in their infant skulls come from *Horrible Histories* and *Newsround*.

Without television, my household's elaborate system of bribes would collapse. My children read books only in response to my frequent threats to take the TV to the dump.

3 Choose two words or phrases from the extract above. Write a sentence commenting on each one's connotations.

....

....

....

Rhetorical devices 1

Read the extract from the online article below (**Source 1**), then answer Questions 1 and 2.

Source 1

Time to let the furry friends go

My daughter is nearly 12. This month she graduated to secondary school and resolved to put childish things behind her. To that end, she lined up her entire menagerie of soft toys on the sofa, five deep, to make a considered, contemplative decision about which of them was going to get the chop.

There were bears, geese, rabbits, dogs, hedgehogs, pigs, elephants, a penguin, two tigers and a single doll, a scraggy female item named, for some reason, Bob. The toys had all featured in her life at one time or another. Large ones, small ones. Sucked ones, chewed ones. Loved ones, unloved ones. Nameless ones.

And now they were huddling together on the sofa like the proud, uncowering victims of a firing squad.

I walked into the living room to see all this just as my daughter, who sat facing them, removed a cupping hand from her chin. She looked solemn.

'What's going on?' I said.

'I'm just deciding which ones to "let go",' she replied, supplying the quote marks with her fingers, and went back to her thinking. For a moment I felt almost physically sick. 'You can't do that!' I said, and then thought, why the hell not? They're hers.

'Why not?' she said. 'They're mine. And besides, I've looked after them all these years. I can do what I want with them.'

I had no answer to that. But it didn't stop me from feeling uneasy.

I told myself that it was because I was upset at the spectacle of my daughter cutting herself away so ruthlessly from her infancy. But I knew that I was not facing up to the whole truth.

1 How many of the following rhetorical devices can you identify in the article? Look for at least **three**, circle them below and label them in the article.

- alliteration
- repetition
- emotive language
- short sentence
- rhetorical question
- lists
- hyperbole

2 For each device you identified, write one or two sentences commenting on:
- why the writer has used it
- its intended effect on the reader.

....

....

....

....

....

....

....

....

....

....

Had a go ☐ Nearly there ☐ Nailed it! ☐

Rhetorical devices 2

Read the extract from the online article below (**Source 1**), then answer Questions 1 and 2.

Source 1

Battery-farmed puppies are a shame on our nation

We are a nation of dog lovers. Or are we?

Linda Goodman is a truly committed dog lover. So much so that, in an attempt to draw attention to the plight of battery-farmed dogs, she has chosen to live like a breeding bitch. A live webcam has been filming her suffering for five days so far. But so far, very few people have paid her much attention.

When we talk of puppy farming, you might imagine it could be quite picturesque – adorable photogenic pups gamboling in paddocks. But it's actually grotesque.

There are estimated to be 5,500 breeding bitches living in council-approved licensed kennels in just three counties of Wales. They will never know the love of a human being, never sit on a sofa, go for a walk, play fetch or have that spot on their tummies tickled that will make their back leg twitch. Enslaved to a breeding schedule, they're just locked in a barn for years and years, left to stand in their own mess – often in the dark – until their litter size falls to an unprofitable size, at which point they are put to sleep.

Why? Because we buy their pups. Their misery will continue until the trade is either banned or it becomes unprofitable. The poor pups, meanwhile, are destined for dealers and pet shops. It's a gamble if they even survive the journey or their first few weeks. The life of a battery-farmed dog is cheap. Their poor rearing, lack of socialisation and lack of health tests can make them expensive for their owners, though.

The Kennel Club estimates one in five of us have bought a puppy-farmed dog. Linda in the shed knows all this. That's why she's locked herself in.

So what can you do to get Goodman and all those poor dogs out of the shed? Write to your MP. And resist the temptation of that puppy in the window, so that it becomes unprofitable to trade in misery.

1 How many of the following rhetorical devices can you identify in the article? Look for at least **three**, circle them below and label them in the article.

- rhetorical question
- lists
- contrast
- repetition
- emotive language
- pattern of three

2 For each device you identified, write one or two sentences commenting on:
- why the writer has used it
- its intended effect on the reader.

....

....

....

....

....

....

....

....

Figurative language

Read **Source 1** below, then answer Question 1.

An answer that **comments on the effect** of figurative language will gain far more marks than one that simply says 'It's a simile' but that does not comment on its effect.

Source 1

A POOR SCHOOL REPORT IS NO BARRIER TO SUCCESS

I hope there are a few red faces at Eton this week. The school prides itself on turning out pupils who will shine in later life, but it made a pig's ear of educating the biologist Professor Sir John Gurdon, who has just been awarded the Nobel Prize (for medicine) for his pioneering work in the field of cloning.

It would be 'a sheer waste of time' for Gurdon to pursue a career in science, wrote his teacher, a Mr Gaddum, in a withering end-of-term report in 1949. He wouldn't listen, couldn't learn simple biological facts and, horror of horrors, 'insisted on doing work in his own way'. In one test, Gurdon scored a miserable 2 out of 50.

1 The writer uses the word 'shine' **figuratively**. What does this metaphor suggest?

....

....

....

Now read the rest of the text, then answer Questions 2 and 3.

One wonders how many other pupils Mr Gaddum and his ilk put off with their caustic one-liners.

Sir John certainly isn't the first high achiever to have had buckets of cold water poured over him by his teachers. 'He will never amount to anything,' predicted a Munich schoolmaster in 1895, failing to spot the potential in the young Albert Einstein. Gary Lineker's teacher warned: 'He must devote less of his time to sport if he wants to be a success – you can't make a living out of football.'

These days, thank goodness, the pendulum has swung the other way. I savoured my daughters' school reports. 'Clara is a legend,' wrote her chemistry teacher when she was 15. Her confidence rocketed – until she compared notes with her friends and found there had been five legends in one class.

Some parents worry that today's schoolchildren would benefit from a few home truths. But they shouldn't miss the obvious moral of Sir John's story. Growing children need encouragement like a plant needs water.

2 Identify at least one more metaphor from the article. Write one or two sentences commenting on why the writer has used it and its effect on the reader.

....

....

....

3 Identify the simile the writer has used in the article. Write one or two sentences commenting on why the writer has used it and its effect on the reader.

....

....

....

Had a go ☐ Nearly there ☐ Nailed it! ☐

Identifying sentence types

Look at the sentences below, then answer the questions that follow.

A My hands were trembling.

B Even though I had done this hundreds of times before, I was still terrified.

C My blood ran cold and my heart stopped.

D Blind terror.

1 Look carefully at the four sentences above. Each one is a different type of sentence. But which is which?

Sentence .... is a simple sentence.

Sentence .... is a compound sentence.

Sentence .... is a complex sentence.

Sentence .... is a minor sentence.

2 Now look at **Source 1** (a newspaper article). Highlight or circle one example of each kind of sentence: simple, compound, complex and minor.

Source 1

No laughing matter

The people of Norwich have an unhappy distinction. They laugh just 5.4 times a day on average, which makes them the most sombre souls in the country. At the other end of the laughometer come the people of Leeds, who push the dial up to 8.7 daily laughs. Sounds impressive. But the boffins warn that even this effort falls well short of the 'healthy benchmark' that is, apparently, 15 laughs a day for adults (pre-school children can get through 400 a day without any trouble).

Does that mean we are gloomier than we used to be? Apparently so. Research suggests that 60 years ago we would spend as much as 18 minutes a day laughing, but that is now down to a paltry 6 minutes. But that would imply that each registered laugh lasts the best part of a minute. Surely nothing is that funny.

- A SIMPLE sentence contains **a subject** and **one verb**, giving **one piece of information** about an event or action.
- A COMPOUND sentence is a series of single sentences joined together. So it contains **two or more verbs**, giving **two or more pieces of information** about events or actions. They are connected with **and** or **but** or **then**.
- A COMPLEX sentence is a longer sentence with one part dependent on another. So it contains **two or more verbs**, giving **two or more pieces of information** about events or actions joined with a range of connecting words, such as **because**, **although**, **if** and several others.
- A MINOR sentence is grammatically incomplete because it does not contain a verb.

Commenting on sentence types

Read the extract from Ben Fogle's autobiography below (**Source 1**), then answer Questions 1 and 2.

Source 1

The accidental adventurer

Shadows danced across the canvas like fiendish ghouls. Their long, clawed fingers scratched menacingly against the fabric. I lay rigid as a gentle breeze snapped at the loose skirt of my tent.

My arms were stretched down my sides, soldier-like, and I lay on my hands to stop them trembling.

What the hell was that deafening noise reverberating around the tent? I held my breath again, but the pounding continued. It was my heart racing with fear. Each beat creating a thunderous din.

I felt faint. This was it. The sleeping bag began to vibrate to the beat of my heart. I had never been so scared in my entire life.

1 The extract begins with two short, simple sentences that describe the scene. What kind of mood do these short sentences create?

....

....

....

2 The extract ends with a series of very short, simple sentences. How do these add to the mood which the writer has created?

....

....

....

Read on, then answer Question 3.

I had to make a run for it. My life depended on it. I needed to wait for the right moment and run as fast as I could. Quietly I eased my body from the bag. My heart began to race even faster.

I'd taken risks, but it was never meant to end like this. Here. Now. I still had so much I wanted to achieve. I hadn't even had a chance to say goodbye.

Guided

3 In this extract, the writer uses a mixture of simple, compound and minor sentences. Write one or two sentences about the effect each of these sentence types creates.

The writer uses several simple and short compound sentences to ....

....

....

....

The use of minor sentences ....

....

....

....

Putting it into practice

Cookery lessons are to be made compulsory for all pupils in England, up to the age of 14. 'About time,' says Esther Walker, who had to teach herself to cook. Read the extract from her newspaper article below (**Source 1**), then have a go at the exam-style question opposite.

Source 1

Four years ago, when I moved in with my husband, Giles, he did all the cooking because I couldn't. I didn't know how. It wasn't out of defiance or a feminist statement, I just didn't know where to start. Giles was – and is – a restaurant critic. He didn't care that I couldn't cook, he was just pleased I wasn't a vegetarian. So he cooked or we ate out.

Despite watching my mother make dinner for no fewer than six people every night for the 25 years I lived at home, I had no idea how she did it. She went shopping every day, bought whatever had a 'reduced' sticker on it and then we ate it for dinner. During the BSE crisis, when beef on the bone was dirt cheap, we ate like kings.

It never occurred to me that cooking was something that you had to learn. I thought that when the time came you would just do it, instinctively. My mother's tranquillity in the kitchen was probably why – she made it seem like making dinner every night, for a full table, was no big deal. She made it look so easy. But my mother didn't teach us how to cook and I didn't ask her to. My mother, although she has no known faults, is not one of life's teachers. She left us to work things out for ourselves. And we – her four daughters – mostly have.

I certainly wasn't taught how to cook at school. I went to a north London grammar in the 90s: the idea that you would teach girls domestic science was abhorrent – what, so we could become kitchen slaves, you chauvinist pig? We were supposed to run companies, be surgeons and other big shots. How they expected us to feed ourselves, let alone anyone else, I don't know. Perhaps they thought we'd be hiring cooks, or our husbands would be doing it, or we'd eat takeaway. Perhaps they assumed we were being taught at home.

The state has now realised that it has failed an entire generation by abandoning this side of their education; it has responded with the School Food Plan, devised by Henry Dimbleby and John Vincent, founders of the restaurant chain Leon, which will make practical cooking compulsory for all pupils in England up to the age of 14. It won't be just designing pizza boxes and discussing the importance of washing your hands, but learning to cook a 'repertoire of savoury meals'. It can't come too soon.

At times I look back on my mother's relentlessly even temper when it came to mealtimes and feel a little bit ashamed. If everyone was taught how to cook at school equally, if cooking was treated as an essential life skill, like learning how to drive or spell, would I – or anyone else – feel the same occasional resentment about it? I learned how to cook by accident but I know a lot of my peers never learned how and probably never will.

I hope that there will still be cooking taught in schools when my children are old enough to learn how; even then, I'll make sure they don't leave home without knowing how to make a stew, roast a chicken and assemble a pie. If I've learned anything over the last five years, it's that dinner is simply too important to be left to chance.

Putting it into practice

4 Explain the different ways in which language is used for effect in the text. Give some examples and analyse what the effects are. *(16 marks)*

When you tackle this kind of question in the exam, remember to:

- spend around 20–25 minutes answering it (remember that in your exam you will be asked to **compare** the ways in which language used in **two** texts, so use this question to practise writing about language in just **one** text)
- read the source text carefully, highlighting any effective language choices
- support all your points with evidence and a clear explanation focusing on **effect**.

Remember: You will have more space than this to answer the question in the exam. Use your own paper to finish your answer to the question above.

Had a go ☐ Nearly there ☐ Nailed it! ☐

Making the best comments

Read the extract from a university student's online blog below (**Source 1**), then answer Questions 1 and 2.

Source 1

Is your Facebook page a lie?

When I started university, people told me: 'These will be the best days of your life.' I was leaving my snoozy town in the countryside and heading towards the sparkle of the big city to study fashion journalism at the London College of Fashion. Not only would these be the best days of my life, everyone said, but also they would be the most glamorous.

They couldn't have been more wrong. By the end of my first year I was seriously considering dropping out. I had not made as many friends, had as much fun, or enjoyed my course as much as I thought I was going to. My shoulders sagged with the weight of my disappointment, and I blamed myself. 'I chose this. Is it my fault I am not living the university dream?' I felt sad and desperately lonely. But I didn't tell anyone.

I certainly didn't put it on Facebook – its culture of competitive sharing made me feel even worse. Scrolling through my friends' feeds, it was clear they were having a ball. Jemma Lamble and I are friends on Facebook – what impression did she get from my profile? 'There is one feeling I got when I clicked on your Facebook and that is jealousy. You looked like you were really enjoying yourself.'

1 Look at the different kinds of comments which one student made on the extract above. Which is which? Draw lines from the type of comment to the correct answer.

1 Comment on viewpoint	**A** The short sentence 'They couldn't have been more wrong' bluntly interrupts the build up of excitement, puncturing it sharply.
2 Comment on purpose	**B** The writer vividly and honestly describes the impact which her disappointment had on her.
3 Comment on language choice	**C** The writer's excitement at heading to university is suddenly undermined when she reveals that it turned out to be a great disappointment.
4 Comment on sentence structure	**D** The physical and emotional impact of the writer's disappointment encourages the reader's sympathy.
5 Comment on the effect on the reader	**E** The word 'sparkle' in strong contrast to 'snoozy' builds up the reader's expectations, making the writer's disappointment seem all the greater.

2 Look again at **Source 1**. Make **two** further comments on the text. Aim to make two different kinds of comment – e.g. on purpose and sentence structure.

....

....

....

....

....

Comment on language and purpose: argue and persuade

Read the extract from a newspaper article below (**Source 1**), then answer Question 1.

Source 1

I'd risk my life to rescue my dog; that's just what owners do

Every winter there are stories of dog owners who have died trying to save a dog that has fallen through ice. People who have no pets of their own often listen to such stories with dismay. Why would anyone risk their life trying to save a dog? I would. Your dog's part of your family, and part of your life. You love it. If you have no family, partner or children, you possibly love your dog even more. It's your companion: a reason to get up in the morning. Your life revolves round it, and if you see it in any sort of serious trouble, then you will, usually, try and save it, just as you would try and save anyone else that you love.

Guided

1 In the extract, the writer uses a rhetorical question followed by a very short sentence. Think about how these language techniques support the writer's argument, and the effect she wants to have on the reader. Write one or two sentences explaining your ideas.

The rhetorical question engages the reader, inviting them to ....

....

....

The short sentence answers the question firmly and emphatically. The effect of this is ....

....

....

Read the final paragraph of the article, then answer Question 2.

I am not expecting that this will convince anyone who's never had a dog. Many people are outraged if you compare an animal to a child. But if a helpless creature that you love is in serious trouble, possibly about to die, it doesn't really matter if it's a dog, a cat, a horse or a beached whale. You're going to go on jumping into rivers, oceans, fights and fires to save it, whatever anyone else thinks.

2 Identify examples of the following language techniques in the paragraph above. Write one or two sentences commenting on the effect of each one.

(a) emotive language: ....

....

....

(b) a list: ....

....

....

Had a go ☐ Nearly there ☐ Nailed it! ☐

Comment on language and purpose: describe

Read the travel writing extract below (**Source 1**), then answer Question 1.

Source 1

Bondi Beach

It is 5.45am. In the dim pre-dawn light a hooded figure slips silently by. He is barefoot and carries a large flat board under his arm. With head bowed, he is walking purposefully. I follow. He pads down the main street under the fig trees, past a row of shops and cafés not yet open.

The hooded man is gliding on and I quicken my pace. Already I can hear the sound of the ocean. We make our way down the stone steps, past the memorial to the Australian dead of two world wars, across the promenade and on to the soft sandy beach. The surf is rolling in. The young man, now bare chested, is running down the beach, splashing through the waves and swimming out. The sea is studded with flotsam, as though a ship has been wrecked. I look again and realise that the black debris is scores of surfers waiting on their boards like praying mantises.

This is Bondi Beach, Australia. The air is still cool and as the sun rises it seems the whole beach begins to move, gyrating and pumping in a fitness frenzy.

Runners, sleek as panthers, are pacing along the promenade and, on the grass, muscles are expanding and contracting rhythmically in the green gym. In the pool at the southern end of the beach swimmers pound up and down in training. This is the other face of Bondi, one of Sydney's most fashionable beaches, which you have to rise early to witness.

1 How many of the following features of **descriptive writing** can you identify and label in the extract?

(a) Descriptions using the five senses.

(b) Figurative language – e.g. simile, metaphor.

(c) Carefully chosen language.

(d) The writer's feelings.

Guided

2 Choose two of these features including the simile underlined. Write one or two sentences about each one, commenting on the writer's choice and its effect on the reader.

The writer uses a simile to compare the waiting surfers with praying mantises. This suggests ....

....

....

....

....

....

....

....

Comment on language and purpose: inform and explain

Read the extract from a newspaper article below (**Source 1**), then answer Question 1.

Source 1

Having friends and going swimming are more important than money to today's youth

In their world of mobile phones, the latest fashions and, of course, Facebook, this may be a tough sell to your stroppy teenager. But it seems it really is the simple things in life that will make them happy.

According to new research, children aged 10–15 gain an increased sense of well-being by having friends around for tea, going swimming and a secure home life rather than a steady flow of money.

Guided

1 How would you describe the tone of this article? Write one or two sentences using evidence from the text to support your ideas.

The tone of the article is ....

....

....

This tone is created through the writer's choice of language – for example, ...

....

....

Read more of the article, then answer Question 2.

Children in families with a lower income were no less happy than those with higher-earning parents, says a study by the Institute for Social and Economic Research at the University of Essex. It found that using the Internet can be beneficial, but only for up to an hour a day as anything more can affect important social activities.

Girls aged between 10 and 12 are the happiest group of children, while those aged 12–15 are the least happy.

Eating five portions of fruit and vegetables a day is also important, the research found.

2 How has the tone of the article changed in these paragraphs? Why has it changed? Write one or two sentences using evidence from the text to support your ideas.

....

....

3 Which of these key features of information and explanation writing can you identify in the extract?

(a) Facts and statistics.

(b) Connective such as **first**, **then**, **next** help to signal the structure of the text.

Write down an example of any that you find, then write a sentence commenting on their effect on the reader.

....

....

Putting it into practice

Read **Source 1** below, then have a go at the exam-style question opposite.

Source 1

A control freak looks for love

MY LAST GIRLFRIEND was a loser. Literally. A wonderful and beautiful person, but prone to losing things; keys, money, credit cards, mobile phones. Each time she lost something, she would get upset and come to me for help and reassurance.

I, on the other hand, am a keeper. Not in the American sense that women throw themselves at me; rather that if you were to ask me to lay my hands on a receipt for a pair of shoes I bought in 1997, I would be angry if it took me more than 90 seconds to locate it. Over to the filing cabinet I would stroll, R for Receipts, S for Shoes, and work through chronologically.

We argued frequently over what she saw as something she was powerless to change, and I saw as a correctable weakness in her character.

In general I would say I find it difficult to accept other people's shortcomings. I am not an unfair person but I do think more effort is the solution to most problems. Not losing things is simply a matter of trying harder to remember where you put them, isn't it?

Wanting things my own way is not something I like about myself. From my love of right angles to my stubborn, black and white views on complex issues, I recognise I can be a very difficult person to be around. I also cannot fail to recognise many symptoms of obsessive-compulsive personality disorder. I have countless habits that I know serve no purpose but am powerless to avoid. I arrange my coins into ascending size in my pockets, for example, and nothing gives me more comfort than the knowledge that my forks, knives and spoons are all in the correct place, tessellating magnificently in their drawer.

My last relationship ended in 2003 (it seems the final thing my girlfriend lost was her desire to put up with my constant nit-picking) and I decided to take a break for a while. There is no reason, I thought, why people can't be completely happy on their own. Initially I revelled in returning home to find that everything was exactly where I had left it; that there was as much milk as there had been when I last used some and that I could watch whatever I wanted on TV. The novelty has now definitely worn off and the grass on the other side of the fence is a sickly, HD green.

When you look into the eyes of the person you love, it is easy to forget that there is anything else in the world besides the river of emotion flowing between you. Why, then, do you want to push them out of the window 5 minutes later for putting a wet teaspoon into the sugar? Have they not been told a thousand times that the sight of the brown clusters this forms makes you feel sick? Of course they have... so they must be doing it because they hate you! You hate them, too. How could you have been so blind earlier? Then, as you are getting up to charge headlong in their direction, they laugh – and you remember why you love them – and the whole exhausting cycle begins anew.

I can't shake off my feeling that the only inevitable result of a long-term relationship is that you will see somebody else's weaknesses and they will see yours. Eventually you will lose respect for one another and either break up or find yourselves locked into a loveless future. Am I right? Of course not! Can I change? I sincerely hope so because, as it stands, it is clearly me who is the loser, desperately looking for a keeper.

Putting it into practice

4 Explain the different ways in which language is used for effect in the text. Give some examples and analyse what the effects are. *(16 marks)*

When you tackle this kind of question in the exam, remember to:

- spend around 20–25 minutes answering it (note that in your exam you will be asked to **compare** the ways in which language used in two texts, so use this question to practise writing about language in just **one** text)
- read the source text carefully, highlighting any effective language choices
- support all your points with evidence and a clear explanation focusing on **effect**.

Remember: You will have more space than this to answer the question in the exam. Use your own paper to finish your answer to the question above.

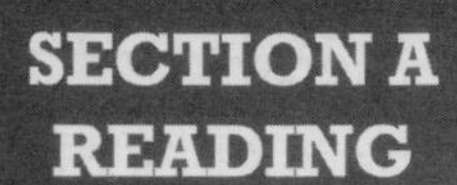

Had a go ☐ Nearly there ☐ Nailed it! ☐

Looking closely at language

Read the newspaper article below (**Source 1**), then answer the questions that follow.

Source 1

On the 12th day of Christmas ... your gift will just be junk

There's nothing they need, nothing they don't own already, nothing they even want. So you buy them an electronic drum-machine T-shirt; a Darth Vader talking piggy bank; an ear-shaped iPhone case; a sonic screwdriver remote control; bacon toothpaste; a dancing dog. They seem amusing on the first day of Christmas, daft on the second, embarrassing on the third. By the twelfth they're in landfill.

Researching her film The Story of Stuff, Annie Leonard discovered that, of the materials flowing through the economy, only 1 per cent remain in use six months after sale. Even the goods we might have expected to hold on to are soon condemned to destruction through either planned obsolescence (wearing out or breaking quickly) or perceived obsolescence (becoming unfashionable). And we are screwing the planet to make them.

Forests are felled to make 'personalised heart-shaped wooden cheese board sets'. Rivers are poisoned to manufacture talking fish. This is pathological consumption: a world-consuming epidemic of collective madness, made so normal by advertising and by the media that we scarcely notice what has happened to us.

Bake them a cake, write them a poem, give them a kiss, tell them a joke, but for God's sake stop trashing the planet to tell someone you care. All it shows is that you don't.

1 (a) What is the **purpose** and **tone** of this text? ....

....

....

(b) Write one or two sentences commenting on how the language used in the article helps to achieve this purpose and create this tone. ....

....

....

....

2 (a) Which language features can you identify in this text? Circle and label as many as you can.

(b) Choose **two** language features and write a sentence about each, commenting on its effect.

....

....

....

....

3 What types and lengths of sentences has the writer used for effect? Choose one and write a sentence commenting on its effect. ....

....

....

Planning to compare language

Read **Sources 1** and **2** below, then complete Question 1.

Source 1

Is it just me?

A friend said something to me recently that gave me pause for thought: 'Miranda, you've got to start taking yourself seriously as a woman.' She said this in response to the frayed, overstuffed handbag – and by handbag I obviously mean rucksack – that I've taken to carrying around with me.

Is it just me who hasn't bought into the need for a £700 designer bag? There is no need when my current rucksack straps on like a dream, giving me a pleasingly, outward-bound Girl Guide-ish look, and can comfortably hold a small dog, a cagoul, chewing-gum, tights, an emergency sandwich, a *London A–Z*, a banana, a box of tissues, a tube of cleansing hand gel, three bottles of water and 15 notebooks. I see it as one of my very finest purchases.

But, no. In the eyes of this friend, my wonderful carrying-sack is apparently an indication that I'm not 'taking myself seriously as a woman'.

Source 2

What does being a dad mean?

I thought I was ready for fatherhood. I was 40, married, and had had enough of the good life to be able to imagine it ending. Yet parenthood still came as a surprise.

My wife was in labour for 35 hours, and for most of that time I was hanging about, offering what support I could. Seeing my wife – usually independent, strong and wilful – left weak, vulnerable and reliant on me was a painful surprise.

A father's role is to hold his partner's hand and weep manly tears at the sight of the new baby arriving. The sight of my wife giving birth was fascinating and freaky, but not tear-inducing: I just didn't feel like crying.

Not only would I tell new fathers not to worry about crying, I would also tell them not to worry if the newborn baby looks decidedly weird. I knew I was meant to think my daughter was the most beautiful thing on the planet. Instead, I found myself staring at her little face, thinking: 'My God, she looks like a tiny alien.'

1 Look at one student's plan for comparing the language and its effects in the two source texts. Add as much detail to the plan as you can, including points, quotations and explanations.

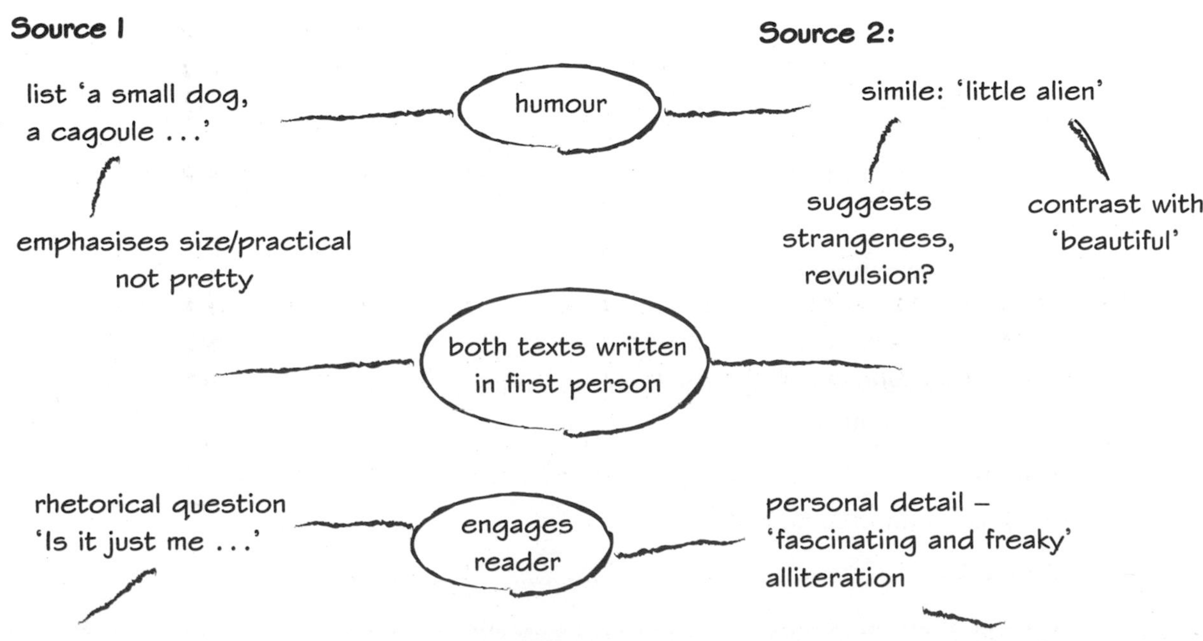

Had a go ☐ Nearly there ☐ Nailed it! ☐

Comparing language

Read **Sources 1** and **2** below, then answer the questions that follow.

Source 1

Splashes of beauty: Kayaking in Kerala

The river holds a mirror image of the sky so accurately in its glassy surface that, save for the occasional insect skittering across the skin, it's hard to distinguish between reality and reflection. A delicate net of wispy clouds stretches across, reining in the hazy outline of mountains wrapped in mist and the emerald green rainforest dipping leafy fingers into the edges.

It's one of those rare moments when it feels as if the earth has been freshly made overnight, emerging from a crisp dawn.

Source 1

Adventure in Wales

If you're an adventure seeker looking for your next destination to conquer, Wales is your answer. Combine some of the UK's highest mountain peaks, striking rugged coastline, seven purpose-built mountain biking centres and the deepest cave in the UK, and you've got a thrilling recipe for an extreme sports experience.

Wales is famous for its mountainous landscape, but it's also one of the best places in Europe to take your first steps underground. There are over 1,000 caves to explore, so there's definitely something to suit all sizes, ages and abilities. Crawl and climb through this secret subterranean world – where narrow tunnels give way to cavernous halls festooned with stalactites and stalagmites – and you'll experience something that surface-dwellers can't even imagine.

1 What are the purposes of the two texts?

(a) The purpose of **Source 1** is to ....

(b) The purpose of **Source 2** is to ....

2 Choose a **short** quotation from each source that shows how each writer's choice of language helps the text achieve its purpose.

Quotation from **Source 1**: ....

....

Quotation from **Source 2**: ....

....

3 Now write a sentence explaining **how** the language in each of your chosen quotations helps the text achieve its purpose.

Source 1: ....

....

Source 2: ....

....

Answering a compare question

When you compare the language used in two texts you can write about:

The content: what the texts are about

Both texts are about ...

On the other hand, **Source 2** explores ...

Source 1 is about ...

The purpose: what they aim to achieve

The purpose of **Source 1** is to ...

Source 2 aims to ...

One way it achieves this through its language choice. For example, ...

The writer's use of language contributes to this through the use of ...

inform | explain | describe | argue | persuade | entertain

The effect on the reader:

Both texts aim to engage the reader but do so in different ways.

Source 1 engages the reader by ...

Source 2, however, uses ...

create humour | influence | shock

Similar language features:

Both texts use rhetorical questions, but use them to achieve different effects.

Source 1 poses the question ...

Source 2 uses a rhetorical question to ...

lists | pattern of three | figurative language | contrast | repetition | emotive language | hyperbole | sentence | structure

1 Look again at the two texts on page 47. Use the prompts above to write a paragraph comparing the different ways in which language is used for effect in the two texts. Remember to give some examples and analyse what the effects are.

....

....

....

....

....

....

Putting it into practice

Read the two sources below, then have a go at the exam-style question on the next page.

Source 1

Lies, damned lies, and teenagers

Anne Korpf

Most teenagers have had plenty of practice in stretching the truth. We adults call it lying, but that's far too blunt for most teenagers.

In my experience teenagers are adept at persuading themselves to believe in the tallest of tales, but what's intriguing is the speed with which even the most transparently honest primary school kid can mutate into a lying teen. Only 5% of undergraduates in an American study said that they never lied to parents, though reassuringly most grow out of it.

Teenagers' task – their job, if you like – is separating from their parents: this involves rejecting, at least temporarily, their parents' values. You could go further and argue that they're trying to spare their parents from the ghastly truth – the excesses that teens consider normal but parents see as a sign that their kids are going off the rails. Seen like this, teenage dishonesty is actually an example of their morality.

The experts advise parents not to try and catch teens out in their lies, force confessions out of them, lecture them or get angry. Are they kidding? My own rules of thumb are rather different. Looking them straight in the eye with as much wry disbelief as you can muster, smile. It's quite hard for them to sustain a fib if they start laughing too. Even if they don't, at least you've proved you're not as easily duped as they believe, or hope.

Source 2

What's it really like to be a teenager?

Ash Moran, 18, Dorset

I live in the middle of nowhere, so going to college in Salisbury was a big thing. When I went to college I wanted to be a hairdresser. I did a course in art and design; now I want to try photography. If that fails I want to work with children. But only when I'm older, like when I'm 40-odd.

The best thing about being a teenager is that life is easy. You've got no worries. You don't need to worry about money because you've got your parents. You're just at school, all you do is just hang out with your mates really. The worst thing is not having freedom because you're stuck at home and you can't really go places. My mum's a single mum – at first if I went to a party she wanted the house phone number, I was like, 'That's ridiculous'. Slowly she's started to trust me more and more, and now she's really relaxed and I'll text her because I respect her. When I have kids I would do it the same way she's done it. I might even ring her for advice.

Putting it into practice

4 Compare the different ways in which language is used for effect in the two texts. Give some examples and analyse the effects. *(16 marks)*

When you tackle this kind of question in the exam, remember to:

- spend around 20–25 minutes answering it
- read both sources carefully, noting effective use of language that helps the text achieve its purpose and get across the writer's viewpoint
- support all your points with evidence and a clear explanation focusing on effect
- use connectives to compare and contrast the two sources, to guide your reader through the similarities and differences you have identified.

Remember: You will have more space than this to answer the question in the exam. Use your own paper to finish your answer to the question above.

Reading the questions

Look closely at the exam-style question below, then answer Questions 1–4.

5 A national newspaper is running a competition inviting school and college students to write an article for a series entitled 'School days are the happiest days of your life'. Write an article in which you describe a school day you particularly enjoyed, and explain why. *(16 marks)*

1 **(a)** Circle the words in the question that suggest the audience you should be writing for.

(b) Write a description of the audience you should write for.

....

....

2 Circle the words that tell you the two different **purposes** your writing should achieve.

3 Circle the words in the question that tell you the **form** in which you should write your answer.

4 Circle the words that tell you the **topic** you should write about.

Now look at another exam-style question, then answer Question 5.

6 All students should complete at least one month's paid work experience before they leave school. Write a letter to your head teacher, arguing **either** *for* **or** *against* this point of view. *(24 marks)*

5 Circle the words in the question that:

(a) suggest the **audience** you should be writing for.

(b) tell you the **purpose** your writing should achieve.

(c) tell you the **form** in which you should write your answer.

(d) tell you the **topic** you should write about.

Read each question carefully, taking note of:
- audience (e.g. adults, students, parents, etc.)
- purpose (e.g. explain, persuade)
- form (e.g. newspaper article, letter)
- topic.

The questions and planning your exam time

In the **Writing** section of your exam you will answer two questions.

- Question 5 asks you to complete a piece of writing to **inform, explain or describe**.
- Question 6 asks you to complete a piece of writing to **persuade** or **argue** a point of view.

Look at the exam-style paper below, then answer the questions that follow.

Section B: Writing

Answer **both** questions in this section.

You are advised to spend about one hour on this section.

---

5 A national newspaper is running a competition, inviting school and college students to write an article for a series entitled 'School days are the happiest days of your life'. Write an article describing a school day which you particularly enjoyed, and explaining why. *(16 marks)*

6 All students should complete at least one month's paid work experience before they leave school. Write a letter to your head teacher, arguing **either** *for* **or** *against* this point of view. *(24 marks)*

1 How long should you spend in total on your answer to Question 5? .... minutes.

2 How long should you spend in total on your answer to Question 6? .... minutes.

3 Complete the table below, writing in the number of minutes you should spend on the three vital stages of answering each question.

How long should you spend ...	Question 5	Question 6
planning your answer to each question?	.... minutes	.... minutes
writing your answer to each question?	.... minutes	.... minutes
checking your answer to each question?	.... minutes	.... minutes

Check the number of marks which each question is worth. It will help you get an idea of how long you should spend on each question.

Writing for an audience

1 Look at the two exam-style tasks below. Which audience are you being asked to write for?

A **6** 'Technology is taking over our lives. We need to spend less time staring at screens and more time talking to each other.' Write an article for your school or college website arguing **either** *for* **or** *against* this point of view. *(24 marks)*

The audience for this task is ....

B **5** A local newspaper is inviting entries for a writing competition, asking young writers to write an extract from their autobiography. Write your entry, describing a memorable event in your life. *(16 marks)*

The audience for this task is ....

2 Think about the kind of language you would use in your answer to Question A above. Which of the opening sentences below would be the most appropriate for this audience? Write one or two sentences explaining your answer.

(a) Some of us spend half our lives gawping at laptops and the telly which I reckon is just like such a waste of time.

(b) When you see a teenager staring at a computer, do not assume that they are wasting their time.

....

....

....

3 Think about the kind of language you would use in your answer to Question B above. Which of the opening sentences below would be the most appropriate for this audience? Write one or two sentences explaining your answer.

(a) When I was about seven, the most amazing thing happened.

(b) Well, the funniest thing I remember from when I was little was the time when my brother really lost his rag with me.

....

....

....

4 Choose one of the exam-style tasks above. Write the first two or three sentences of your answer, focusing on using the most appropriate language for your audience.

....

....

....

....

....

Writing for a purpose: inform and explain

Look at the exam-style question below, then answer the questions that follow.

> **5** Many people have a role model – a person whose achievements and attitude they admire. Write an article for your school or college website, informing readers about your role model, and explaining why you chose them. *(16 marks)*

Guided

1 Writing that informs or explains often uses subheadings. Write down up to five subheadings that you could use to organise your answer to the exam-style question above.

1 What's so great about ... .

2 ....

3 ....

4 ....

5 ....

2 Writing that informs or explains often uses facts and statistics to support its ideas and make the reader feel the information is reliable and trustworthy. Write down five facts or statistics that you could include in your writing about your chosen role model.

1 ....

2 ....

3 ....

4 ....

5 ....

3 Writing that informs or explains usually uses a formal tone. It makes your writing seem more reliable and trustworthy. Write the opening paragraph of your response to the exam-style task above. Aim to:

- use a formal tone
- include some of the facts and statistics you used in your answer to Question 2.

....

....

....

....

....

....

....

....

Writing for a purpose: describe

Look at the exam-style question below, then answer the questions that follow.

5 A local interior design company are running a competition asking people to write about their ideal home for their new brochure. Write an entry describing your ideal home. *(16 marks)*

1 Using the five senses can help you to create a vivid image in the reader's mind. Choose one room in your ideal home, then complete the table below to gather ideas you could use in your writing.

In this room, I can ...

see:	
hear:	
smell:	
touch:	
taste:	

2 Figurative language will also help you to create a strong description. Focus on one object in your chosen room. Write one or two sentences, describing it with either a simile, a metaphor or personification.

....

....

....

3 **(a)** How does being in this room make you feel? ....

....

(b) When you feel frightened, you might feel shaky, or sick or sweaty. How does the feeling you chose in Question 3 (a) actually **feel**? Write down three examples:

Example 1: ....

Example 2: ....

Example 3: ....

4 Using your answers to Questions 1, 2 and 3, write the first three sentences of your answer to the exam-style question above.

....

....

....

5 Look at your answer to Question 4. Have you chosen the most precise and vivid descriptive language throughout? If not, choose three words or phrases and consider replacing them with more effective choices.

Writing for a purpose: argue and persuade

Look at the exam-style question below, then answer the questions that follow.

> **6** 'The Internet is an additive and harmful drug.' Write an article for your local newspaper, arguing **either** *for* **or** *against* this point of view. *(24 marks)*

1 When you write to argue, you need at least **three** key points to support your argument. Write down **three** points in support of your argument, either for or against this point of view.

Point 1: ....

Point 2: ....

Point 3: ....

2 You will need to select evidence to support each of your key points. Write down one piece of evidence to support each of the three ideas you noted in your answer to Question 1.

Evidence for Point 1: ....

Evidence for Point 2: ....

Evidence for Point 3: ....

Evidence can be any of these things:
- a fact or statistic
- an expert opinion
- an example from your own experience.

3 Look at the rhetorical devices below. These devices can make an effective argument more powerful:
- rhetorical questions
- direct address
- repetition
- emotive language
- alliteration
- contrast
- patterns of three
- lists
- hyperbole.

Now write **two** sentences that you could include in your answer to the above exam-style question using a rhetorical device in each one.

Sentence 1: ....

Sentence 2: ....

Guided

4 A counter-argument allows you to identify an argument which people might use to disagree with your point of view – which you can then dismiss. What point might people on the opposing side of this argument make? How could you dismiss it? Write your ideas down.

It could be argued that ....

However, ...

....

....

....

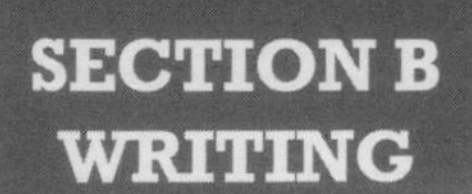

Putting it into practice

Look closely at the exam-style paper below, then answer the questions that follow.

Section B: Writing

Answer **both** questions in this section.

You are advised to spend about one hour on this section.

---

5 Your school or college is inviting entries for a writing competition. The winning entries will be posted on the school or college website. The topic is 'The most important thing I learned at school'. Write your article, informing the reader about the most important thing you learned at school and explaining why you think it is important. *(16 marks)*

6 'Men and women can never be equal.' Write an article for your local newspaper, arguing **either** *for* **or** *against* this point of view. *(24 marks)*

1 How long will you spend on each question?

Q5: .... minutes.

Q6: .... minutes.

Guided

2 Read the questions on the exam paper very carefully, then complete the table below.

	Audience	Purpose	Form	Topic
Question 5	teachers/students			
Question 6		argue		

3 Note down some of the key features you should remember to use in each question.

Question 5: Key features	Question 6: Key features

Form: letters and emails

Look at the extract from an exam-style question below, then complete Questions 1 and 2.

6 Write a letter to the head of your school or college, arguing **either** *for* **or** *against changing the school uniform.* *(24 marks)*

1 It is important to use the correct layout at the beginning and end of a formal letter. Add the following features, correctly laid out, to the letter below:

- your address
- the address of the person you are writing to
- the date
- the salutation (Dear …)
- the sign off (Yours …)
- your signature
- your name.

I am writing regarding your recent letter to parents and students, dated 13 September

and hope you will consider this before making any decision.

2 Which layout features would you **not** need to include if you were asked to write a formal email to the head of your college or school?

....

....

Form: articles

Look at the exam-style question below, then answer the questions that follow.

6 'Many people find teenagers frightening or intimidating – and with good reason.' Write an article for your local newspaper which persuades your readers that this statement is **either** *right* **or** *wrong*. *(24 marks)*

1 Think of a title you could use as your article's **headline**.

....

....

Headlines use a range of techniques including: repetition, a rhetorical question, alliteration, a pun or a rhyme.

2 Think of a **subheading** that will add more information to your headline.

....

....

3 Write your opening paragraph, summing up your ideas in two or three sentences.

....

....

....

....

....

4 Articles often include quotations from 'experts' to support the writer's ideas. You may need to make this up in the exam! Who could you quote in this article? What will they say?

....

....

....

....

....

....

5 Write your closing paragraph concluding your article with your views on the statement.

....

....

....

....

....

....

Form: information sheets

Read the exam-style question below, then answer the questions that follow.

5 Write an information sheet, informing visitors about one aspect or feature of your local area.
(16 marks)

1 Think of two different aspects or features of your local area that you could write about. Then choose the best one.

Aspect/feature 1: ....

Aspect/feature 2: ....

2 Your information sheet will need a title to grab and engage the interest of your readers. Think of **two** possible titles for your information sheet. Then choose the best one.

Title 1: ....

Title 2: ....

3 Organising your writing under subheadings can help guide the reader – and help you to plan your writing. Write down five subheadings you would use in your information sheet.

Subheading 1: ....

Subheading 2: ....

Subheading 3: ....

Subheading 4: ....

Subheading 5: ....

4 Information sheets often use a range of structural features to present information more clearly and appealingly. Which of the following could you include in this leaflet? Write a sentence explaining how you would use them.

Bullet pointed or numbered list: ....

....

Table: ....

....

Chart: ....

....

Text box: ....

....

Putting it into practice

Answer the exam-style question below, focusing in particular on audience, purpose and form.

6 'Students work hard all day at school. They should not have to do homework as well.' Write a letter to the head of your school or college, persuading them that this statement is **either** *right* **or** *wrong*. *(24 marks)*

When you tackle any writing question in the exam, remember to:

- be sure about the audience, purpose, form and topic for your writing
- include all the relevant key features of form and purpose
- plan your writing before you start
- check your spelling, punctuation and grammar thoroughly when you have finished writing.

Remember: You will have more space than this to answer the question in the exam. Use your own paper to finish your answer to the question above.

Planning an answer: describe

Look at the exam-style question below, then answer Question 1.

5 Your school or college is inviting entries for a writing competition. The topic is 'The trip of a lifetime'. Write your entry, describing a memorable trip or holiday. *(16 marks)*

1 Complete the stages of planning outlined below.

Stage 1: Decide which trip or holiday will describe. Write it in the centre of the spidergram below.

Stage 2: You will need to write three or four paragraphs for your answer. Decide what you will include in each one. Add your ideas to the spidergram below.

Stage 3: Add some detail for each of your planned paragraphs. Think about how you could use:

- the five senses: see, hear, smell, touch and taste
- your feelings
- details to create mood or atmosphere
- language for effect.

Your idea **does not** have to be action packed.
It **does not** have to be true.
It **does** have to be written interestingly and engagingly.

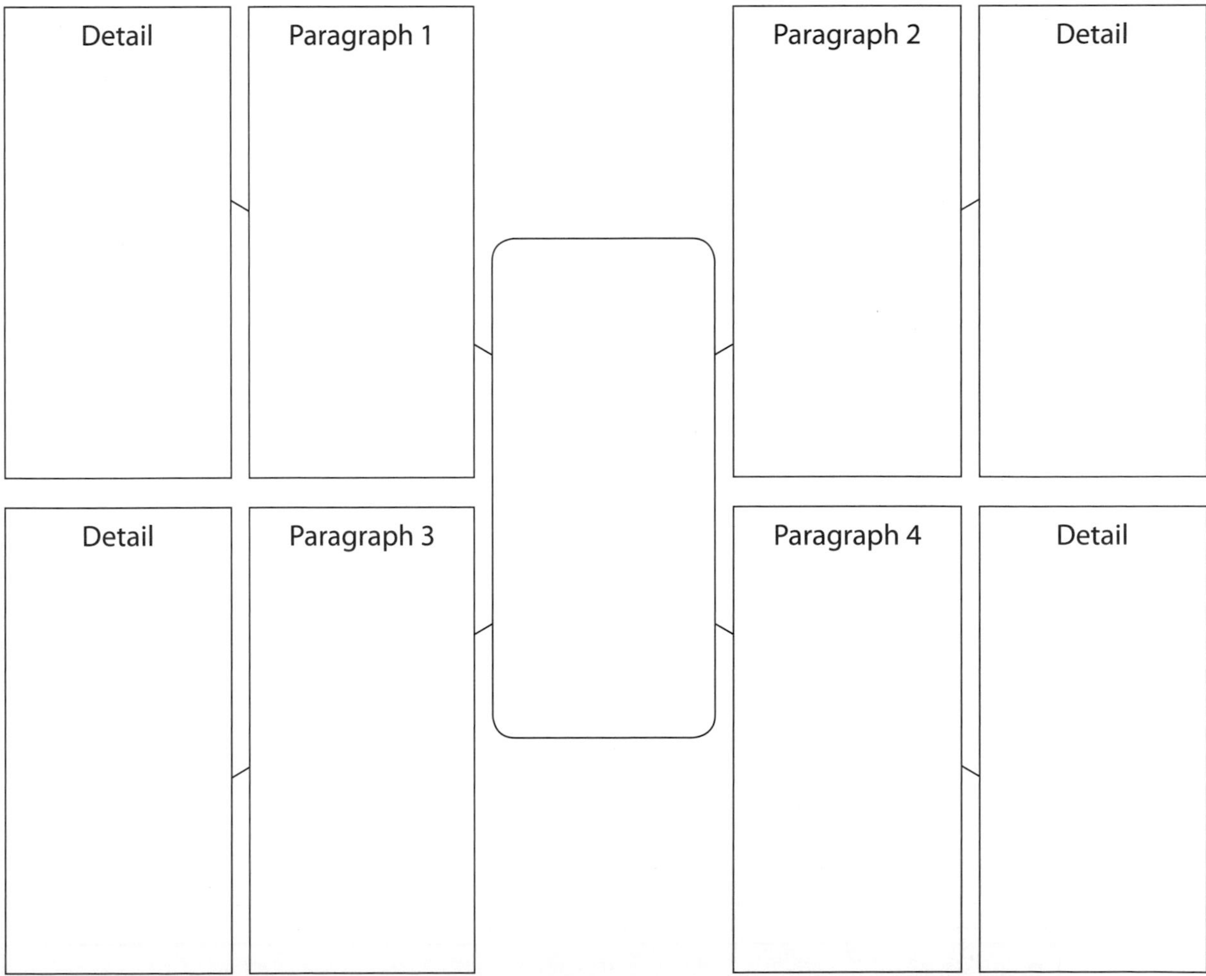

Remember:

- you only have **25 minutes** to plan, write and check this task – so aim for three or four paragraphs of well-crafted writing
- quality is rewarded; quantity is not.

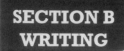

Planning an answer: inform or explain

Look at the exam-style question below, then answer Question 1.

5 A national newspaper is inviting teenagers to contribute to a series of articles. The title of the series is 'One thing I know'. Write your article, offering teenagers one piece of advice and explaining your choice. *(16 marks)*

1 Complete the stages of planning outlined below.

Stage 1: Decide which one piece of advice you would give to teenagers. Write it in the centre of the spidergram below.

Stage 2: To guide your reader, plan an introduction which tells them what are you writing and why they should read it. Add it to the spidergram.

Stage 3: You will need to write three or four paragraphs for your answer. Decide on the key points you will include in each one. You could think of them as subheadings which will help to organise your writing.

Stage 4: Sequence your key points by numbering them. What would be the most logical or effective order?

Stage 5: Add some ideas and details to each of your key points.

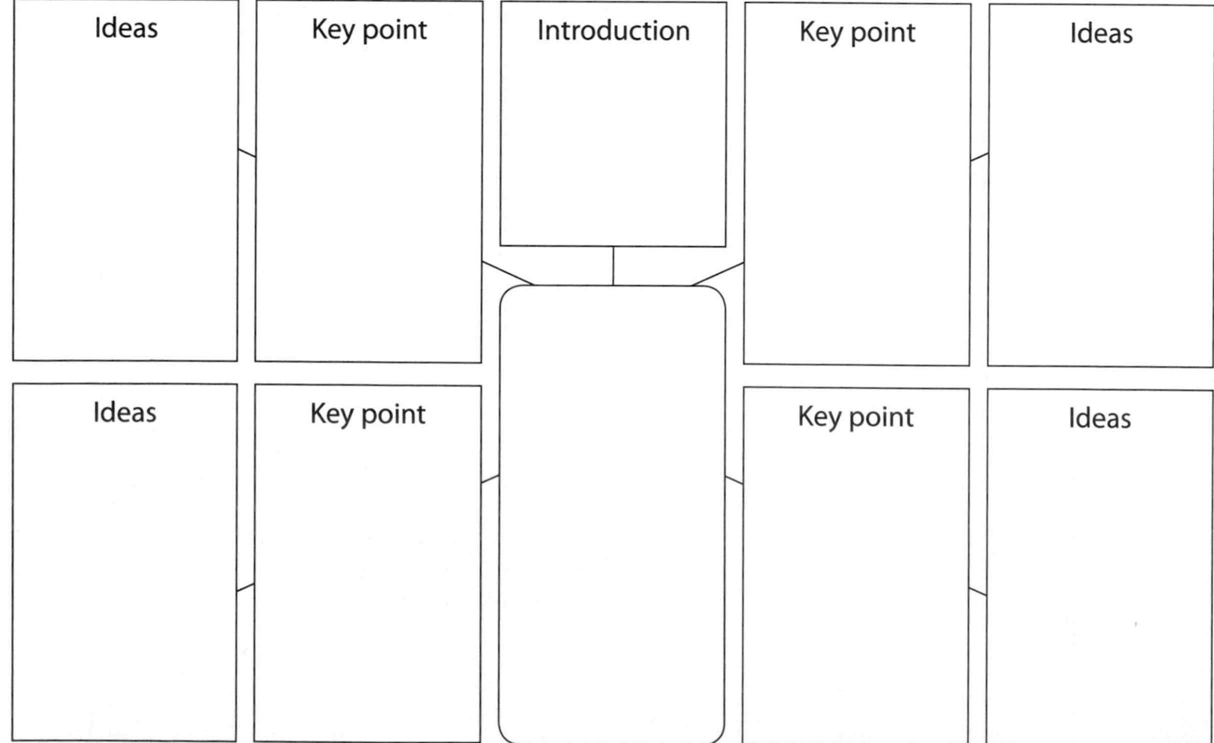

Remember:
- you only have **25 minutes** to plan, write and check this task – so aim for three or four paragraphs of well-crafted writing
- quality is rewarded – quantity is not
- you will not always include subheadings when you write an information or explanation text – but you can still use them to help you plan your writing.

Planning an answer: argue or persuade

Look at the exam-style question below, then answer Question 1.

6 Your local newspaper has been publishing a series of articles on the future of GCSEs. A recent article suggested that exams do not give a fair or accurate picture of a student's real skills and abilities. Write a letter to the editor arguing **either** *for* **or** *against* this point of view. *(24 marks)*

1 Complete the stages of planning outlined below.

Stage 1: Decide whether you agree or disagree with the point of view in the question. Summarise your response in the centre of the spidergram below.

Stage 2: To guide readers, plan an introduction that tells them what are you writing and why they should read it. Add it to the spidergram.

Stage 3: Decide on the **three** key points you will make.

Stage 4: Decide on the evidence you will use to support your key points.

Stage 5: Sequence your key points by numbering them. What would be the most logical or effective order?

Stage 6: Add a counter-argument to your plan. What might someone who opposed your opinion argue? How can you dismiss their argument?

Stage 7: Plan a conclusion that will hammer your point of view home.

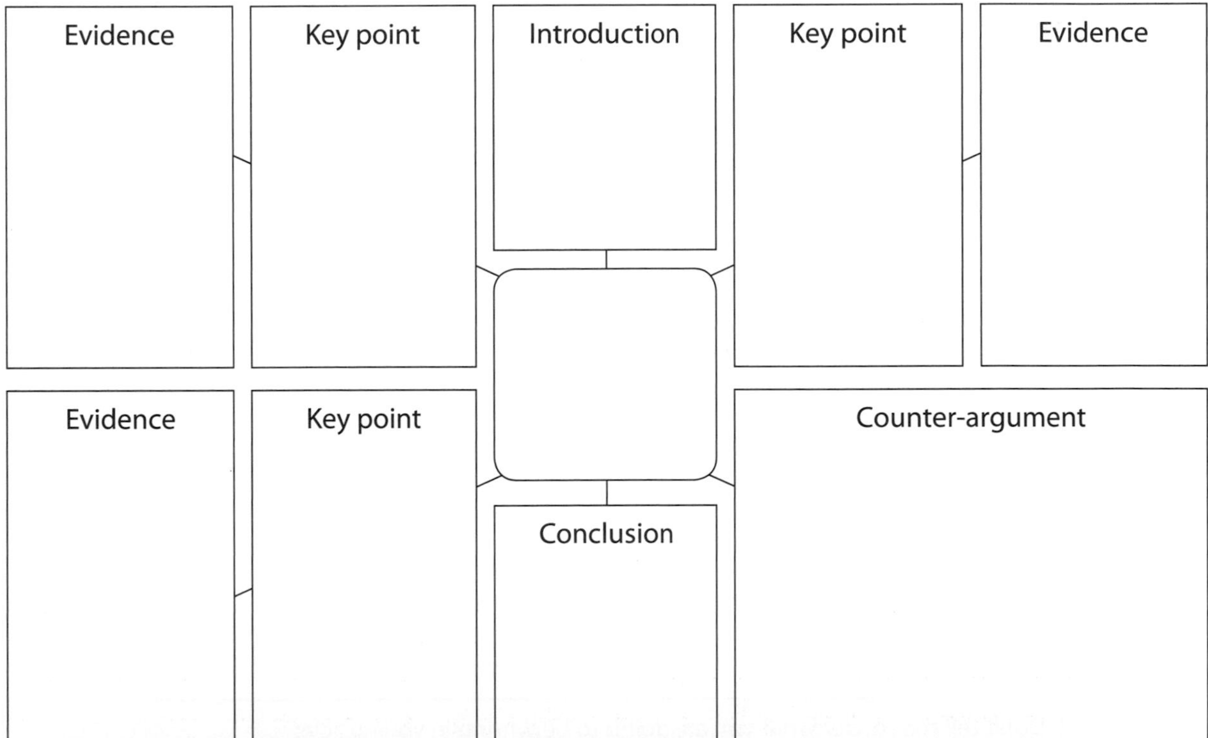

Remember:
- you only have **35 minutes** to plan, write and check this task – so aim for six paragraphs of well crafted writing
- quality is rewarded – quantity is not.

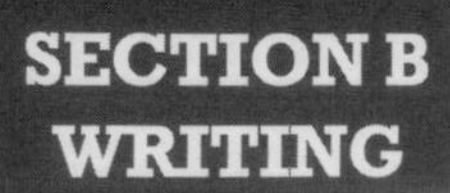

Had a go ☐ Nearly there ☐ Nailed it! ☐

Beginnings

Look at the exam-style question below, then complete the questions that follow.

> **6** 'Schools and colleges should give students more careers advice to help them make the best choices.' Write an article for a magazine of your choice arguing **either** *for* **or** *against* this view.
> *(24 marks)*

1 The first sentences of your writing must grab the reader's attention and make them want to read on. Try writing the opening sentence of your response to the exam-style question above in lots of different ways:

Using a rhetorical question: ....

....

Making a bold or controversial statement: ....

....

With a relevant quotation: ....

....

With a shocking or surprising fact or statistic: ....

....

With a short, relevant, **interesting** anecdote: ....

....

2 Choose one or two of your ideas from Question 1 and write the rest of your introduction to the exam-style question above. Remember you introduction needs to introduce:

- the topic you are writing about
- your argument.

....

....

....

....

....

....

....

Don't tell the reader what you are going to be writing in your article:

In this article I am going to argue that ... ✗

Just write it!

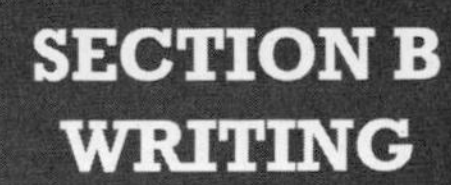

Endings

Look at the exam-style question below, then complete the questions that follow.

6 'Schools and colleges should give students more careers advice to help them make the best choices.' Write an article for a magazine of your choice arguing **either** *for* **or** *against* this view.
(24 marks)

1 The final paragraph or **conclusion** of your writing should make a lasting impression. Try writing sentences you could include in your conclusion to the above exam-style question, using these techniques:

End on a vivid image: ....

....

End on a warning: ....

....

End on a happy note: ....

....

End on a thought-provoking question: ....

....

End on a 'call to action': ....

....

Refer back to your introduction, but don't repeat it: ....

....

2 Choose one or two of your ideas from Question 1 and write your conclusion to the exam-style question above.

....

....

....

....

....

....

....

....

....

....

....

Avoid introducing your conclusion with phrases like:
- In conclusion …
- To summarise …

Putting it into practice

Plan your answer to the exam-style question below.

6 'If the universe is infinite, there must be alien life out there somewhere.' Write an article for your school or college website arguing **either** *for* **or** *against* this point of view. *(24 marks)*

When you tackle any writing question in the exam, remember to:
- be sure about the audience, purpose, form and topic for your writing
- spend 3–5 minutes gathering ideas
- organise and sequence your ideas
- plan how you will introduce and conclude your writing.

Remember: You will have more space than this to answer the question in the exam. Use your own paper to finish your answer to the question above.

Paragraphing

Look at the exam-style question below, then answer the questions that follow.

6 'Schools and colleges should give students more careers advice to help them make the best choices.' Write an article for a magazine of your choice arguing **either** *for* **or** *against* this view.
(24 marks)

1 Look at the paragraph below. It is an extract from one student's response to the exam-style question above.

> When students choose their GCSE options in Year Nine, they do not always choose subjects because they will help them in their future career. I chose my GCSEs either because I liked the teacher or because lots of my friends had chosen that subject. Neither of these reasons are sound. With more advice on the careers available to us and the different ways we can prepare for them, students would make more informed and more sensible decisions.

This student has organised the paragraphs in her argument using Point-Evidence-Explain. Identify and label the three different sections of this paragraph: **point**, **evidence** and **explain**.

2 Plan your own Point-Evidence-Explain paragraph in answer to the above exam-style question.

Point: ....

Evidence: ....

Explain: ....

3 Now write the paragraph you have planned in full.

....

....

....

....

....

....

....

....

....

4 Identify and label the three different sections of your paragraph: **point**, **evidence** and **explain**.

5 Plan a second Point-Evidence-Explain paragraph in answer to the above exam-style question.

Point: ....

Evidence: ....

Explain: ....

Each time you start a new point, start a new paragraph.

Had a go ☐ Nearly there ☐ Nailed it! ☐

Using connectives

1 Different connectives have different purposes. Copy the list of connectives below into the table, adding each one to the correct column.

Because
Consequently
Especially
For example
For instance
Furthermore …
However
In addition …
In particular
In the same way
Moreover …
Not only … but also
On the other hand
Significantly
Similarly
Such as
Therefore
… whereas …

Adding an idea	Explaining	Illustrating	Emphasising	Comparing	Contrasting

2 Look at the paragraphs below. They are extracts from one student's writing on the topic.

… exams do not give a fair or accurate picture of a student's real skills and abilities.

Fill in all the gaps using appropriate connectives.

Many students are enormously successful in areas which exams do not or cannot assess. ...., one student at my school runs his own business designing websites for local companies. This is not something he has learned at school and .... his success will not be reflected in his exam results.

........................, some students' success depends not on hard work but on natural ability. .... this has more impact on less academic students. One student, ..., might achieve an A grade with little or no hard work, while another might have worked solidly and consistently for years to achieve a 'C'.

.... there is no obvious alternative to exams as a measure of students' ability

3 Now write your own Point-Evidence-Explain paragraph in response to the above exam-style question. Remember to use a range of connectives to guide the reader through your argument.

Look back at your planning on page 65 to help you.

....

....

....

....

Putting it into practice

Answer the exam-style question below, focusing in particular on paragraphing and using connectives.

5 What do you think is the greatest invention in the history of mankind? Write an article for your school or college website, informing the reader about your chosen invention and explaining why you chose it. *(16 marks)*

When you tackle any writing question in the exam, remember to:
- write in paragraphs
- plan one point per paragraph
- use connectives to guide your reader through the text.

Remember: You will have more space than this to answer the question in the exam. Use your own paper to finish your answer to the question above.

Had a go ☐ Nearly there ☐ Nailed it! ☐

Getting the right tone

Look at the two exam-style questions below, then answer the questions that follow.

A **6** 'Computer games have no value. They encourage young people to spend hours wasting time that could be spent much more usefully.' Write an article for your school or college website, arguing **either** *for* **or** *against* this view. *(24 marks)*

B **6** 'Computer games have no value. They encourage young people to spend hours wasting time that could be spent much more usefully.' Write an article for a teenage gaming website arguing **either** *for* **or** *against* this view. *(24 marks)*

1 Who is the audience for Question A? ....

2 What kind of tone should you use to appeal to this audience? ...

....

3 Who is the audience for Question B? ....

Formal and informal language, standard English, slang, humour and point of view can all affect the tone of your writing. Think about the audience you are writing for and make your choice.

4 What kind of tone should you use to appeal to this audience? ....

....

5 Look at the sentences below. Which have a tone that would be appropriate for which exam question? Label each sentence either 'A', 'B', or 'N' (for neither).

Point of view: first or third person

Many people think that computer games are designed to empty young people's minds and fill their time

I think computer games have a number of benefits for everyone, young or old.

Formal or informal

It could be argued that some games not only improve the player's problem solving skills but, played collaboratively online, can also develop the ability to work in a team.

It's only oldies and people who don't know their Xbox from their Wii that come up with this sort of argument.

Standard English or non-standard English

What is wrong with switching off your brain and turning on your games console?

There ain't nothing like a session onyer favourite shoot em up to chill you out.

6 Write one or two sentences in response to each of the exam-style questions above.

A ....

....

B ....

....

Synonyms

1 Look at the sentence below. Think of **at least two** synonyms (words with a similar meaning) for each circled word.

Synonyms for 'students':

1 ....

2 ....

3 ....

Synonyms for 'improve':

1 ....

2 ....

3 ....

Students can improve their learning by doing more revision.

Synonyms for 'learning':

1 ....

2 ....

3 ....

Synonyms for 'doing':

1 ....

2 ....

3 ....

If you get stuck, use a thesaurus – but first **TRY** to use the large vocabulary that you already have in your head. Remember, you won't have access to a thesaurus in the exam.

2 Look at each of the words in the table below. Complete the table adding at least two synonyms for each word.

embarrassed	upset	scream	moment	annoyed

3 Now write a paragraph in response to the exam-style question below. Aim to use some of the vocabulary from your answer to Question 2.

5 Your school is inviting entries for a writing competition. The topic is 'My most embarrassing moment'. Write your entry, describing a time when you were embarrassed and explaining why. *(16 marks)*

....

....

....

....

....

....

....

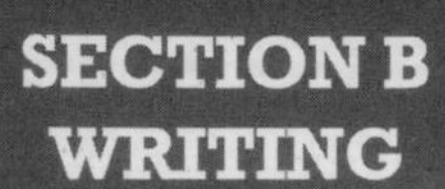

Had a go ☐ Nearly there ☐ Nailed it! ☐

Choosing vocabulary for effect: describe

1 Look at this description.

> The sun's glorious golden rays burst through my gleaming windows, sending shimmering sparkling beams of incandescence dancing around my walls.

Rewrite the above description in **eight** words or fewer. You could re-use some of the original vocabulary or use some of your own ideas.

....

....

2 Look again at your answer to Question 1. Compare your shorter sentence with the longer original version. Which do you prefer? Write a sentence explaining why.

....

....

....

Now look at the exam-style question below, then answer Questions 3 and 4.

> **5** A national newspaper is inviting entries for a writing competition. The topic is 'The greatest place on earth'. Write your entry, describing a place you have particularly enjoyed visiting. It could be somewhere abroad, in the UK, or even in your local area. *(16 marks)*

3 Write two or three sentences in which you begin to describe what you consider to the 'greatest place on earth'.

....

....

....

....

....

....

4 Look again at your answer to Question 3. Have you included enough description? Or too much? Do you need to add more? Or should you cross some out?

5 Look again at your improved answer to Question 3. Circle three words that you think could be improved. Write down three synonyms for each word, then choose the most effective one.

....	....	....
....	....	....
....	....	....

Choosing vocabulary for effect: argue and persuade

Guided

1 Look at the sentences below. Rewrite them, using emotive language to add more impact.

usually? frequently? barbarically? cruelly? destroyed? slaughtered?

A Animals in laboratories are ~~often~~ treated ~~really badly~~ and then ~~put to sleep.~~

B If we continue to use too many of the earth's resources, the world will not have enough food.

C Our lives are filled with computers. We may not like it but we cannot do much about it.

2 Look at this sentence:

Some parents greeted the school's controversial plans with a (cry) of disapproval.

What would be the impact of replacing the circled word with roar ? How would the connotations of roar affect the reader's response to the sentence? Write one or two sentences explaining your ideas.

....

....

....

3 What would be the impact of replacing the circled word with each of these:

howl :...

....

whimper :...

....

4 Write the opening two or three sentences of your answer to the exam question below. Aim to choose vocabulary for its impact and its connotations.

6 'Social networking is a waste of time.' Write an article arguing **either** *for* **or** *against* this view. *(24 marks)*

....

....

....

Had a go ☐ Nearly there ☐ Nailed it! ☐

Language for effect 1

1 Look at the extracts from students' writing below. Some are taken from a piece of descriptive writing, some from a piece of argument writing. Connect the rhetorical devices to the extracts in which they are used.

- contrast
- rhetorical question
- repetition
- list

A Why was he staring at me like that?

B How would you feel if it were your beloved dog or cat being treated in this way?

C Some people carefully sort their rubbish into recycling bins, separating their metal, card, paper, plastic and glass. Most people just chuck it all in one big bin.

D As the phone rang, the bright sunshine disappeared, swallowed by a wall of rolling dark clouds.

E I stared at the crowd in front of me: thin people, fat people, tall people, short people, old people, young people. I recognised none of them.

F The only solution which we should consider, the only solution which the human race can offer, the only solution which we can all contribute to, is right under our noses.

2 Now look at the exam-style question below. Write **up to four** short extracts from your answer, using **one or more** of these language techniques in **each**.

> **6** 'Many adults see teenagers as a problem – but it isn't the teenagers that need to change. It's the adults.' Write an article for a magazine of your choice, arguing **either** *for* **or** *against* this view. *(24 marks)*

....

....

....

....

....

....

....

....

Don't use these language devices as a tick list in the exam, aiming to include one of each in both of your answers. **Do** look for opportunities where they will add to the impact of your ideas.

Language for effect 2

1 Look at the extracts from students' writing below. Some are taken from a piece of descriptive writing, some from a piece of argument writing. Connect the rhetorical devices to the extracts in which they are used.

direct address

pattern of three

alliteration

hyperbole

A For about the hundredth time that day, my sister started sobbing.

B How would you feel if it were your beloved dog or cat being treated in this way?

C The city stretched before me, dark, dangerous and disturbing.

D This is an appalling waste of money. We might as well be setting light to wads of ten pound notes and laughing as we do it.

E We must act intelligently, decisively and immediately.

F Don't just sit there! Get off the sofa and do something.

2 Now look at the exam-style question below. Write **up to four** short extracts from your answer, using **one or more** of these language techniques in **each**.

> 5 Your school or college is inviting entries for a writing competition. The topic is 'Regrets'. Write your entry, describing a time when you regretted something you had done, or a decision you had made, and explaining why. *(16 marks)*

Don't use these language devices as a tick list in the exam, aiming to include one of each in both of your answers. **Do** look for opportunities where they will add to the impact of your ideas.

Had a go ☐ Nearly there ☐ Nailed it! ☐

Language for effect 3

1 Look at the examples of figurative language used in the sentences below. The writers have used similes, metaphors and personification to give their writing impact. But which sentence uses which technique? Circle the correct answer.

A The wind sang in the trees and the branches waved. — simile metaphor personification

B The school has a challenging task ahead – an Everest to be climbed. — simile metaphor personification

C She smiled like a tiger, licking its lips at the sight of a lost child. — simile metaphor personification

D Waiting for the exams to begin is like waiting on death row. — simile metaphor personification

E Homework is a ball and chain around every students' ankle. — simile metaphor personification

F It's at that moment that your completely empty revision timetable creeps up behind you, taps you on the shoulder and asks if it could 'have a word'. — simile metaphor personification

2 Now look at the exam-style question below. Write **up to four** short extracts from your answer, using **one** of these language techniques in **each**.

> **6** Write an article for your school or college website arguing that students can do a great deal to make their school or college a better, cleaner, more inviting place to be. *(24 marks)*

....

....

....

....

....

....

....

....

....

....

Don't try to use one simile, one metaphor and one personification in both of your answers.
Do look for opportunities where they will add impact to your ideas.
Do avoid clichés and be original.

Putting it into practice

Answer the exam-style question below, focusing in particular on language for effect and language devices.

5 Many people are nervous of trying new things: new food, new activities, new places. Describe a time when you tried something new – and explain why you were glad, or sorry, that you did. Your piece will appear in the *Teenage Voices* section of your local newspaper. *(16 marks)*

When you tackle any writing question in the exam, remember to:
- be sure about the audience, purpose, form and topic for your writing
- spend 3–5 minutes gathering ideas
- organise and sequence your ideas
- select language and use language devices for effect in your writing.

Remember: You will have more space than this to answer the question in the exam. Use your own paper to finish your answer to the question above.

Had a go ☐ Nearly there ☐ Nailed it! ☐

Sentence variety 1

Guided

1 Look at the sentences below and identify the sentence type. Are they:

- a simple sentence
- a compound sentence
- a complex sentence
- a minor sentence?

For each one, write a sentence explaining how you know which sentence type it is.

A We must act now because soon it may be too late. This is a .... sentence because ....

B Surely not. This is a .... sentence because ....

C I hurried but I was too late. This is a .... sentence because ....

....

D The time has come. This is a .... sentence because ....

....

Now look at the exam-style question below, then answer Questions 2 and 3.

> **6** 'Sportsmen and women set an extremely bad example. They are liars, cheaters and fakers.' Write an article for a magazine of your choice, arguing **either** *for* **or** *against* this view.
>
> *(24 marks)*

2 Look at the extract from one student's answer to the above exam-style question. It is entirely written in short simple sentences. Rewrite the extract, aiming to use a variety of all four different sentence types.

> Professional footballers are possibly the worst 'fakers'. With just one tap from another player they fall over. Sometimes they dive to the ground. Occasionally they fly. They always start screaming. It shows they are seriously injured. They say it was a foul. They demand a free kick. It is ridiculous.

3 Write your own short paragraph in response to the above exam-style question, aiming to use a variety of all four different sentence types.

....

....

....

....

....

....

....

Sentence variety 2

Look at the exam-style question below, then answer Questions 1 and 2.

5 A national newspaper is inviting entries for a writing competition. The topic is 'City life or country life?' Write your entry, explaining why you would rather live in a city or in the countryside. *(16 marks)*

Guided

1 Write a sentence that you could use in your answer to the above exam-style question, beginning with:

(a) a pronoun (e.g. I, he, she, they): I grew up in a tiny village in the middle of nowhere.

(b) an article (e.g. a, an, the): ....

....

(c) a preposition (e.g. above, behind, between): ....

....

(d) an -ing word (or present participle) (e.g. running, hurrying, crawling): ....

....

(e) an adjective (e.g. slow, quiet, violent): ....

....

(f) an adverb (e.g. alarmingly, painfully, happily): ....

....

(g) a connective (subordinating clause + main clause) (e.g. if, although, because): ....

....

2 Now write a paragraph in response to the above exam-style question. Aim to use:

- all seven different types of sentence opener in your writing
- a different word to start each of your sentences.

....

....

....

....

....

....

....

....

....

....

....

Had a go ☐ Nearly there ☐ Nailed it! ☐

Sentences for effect

1 Look at the sentences below. What effect is the long sentence followed by the short sentence intended to have on the reader?

> The ladder tipped over, the paint pot went flying, the paint exploded over her sofa, the paint pot hit her treasured vase, and the vase smashed into dust. I froze.

The effect of the long sentence is: ....

....

The effect of the short sentence is: ....

....

Guided

2 Now look at the three sentences below. Notice how the same ideas have been used, but in a different order.

A Before I walked the six miles home, I scrubbed every last drop of paint from the carpet and swept up every last crumb of glass, while she watched with a grim smile of quiet satisfaction on her lips.

B While she watched with a grim smile of quiet satisfaction on her lips, I scrubbed every last drop of paint from the carpet and swept up every last crumb of glass before I walked the six miles home.

C Before I walked the six miles home, she watched with a grim smile of quiet satisfaction on her lips while I scrubbed every last drop of paint from the carpet and swept up every last crumb of glass.

How does the order in which the information is organised affect each sentence's emphasis?

The first sentence emphasises ....

....

....

....

3 Now write the opening two or three sentences of your own response to the exam-style question below. Aim to include a:

- long sentence followed by a short sentence
- sentence structured to give specific emphasis.

> **5** Write an article for a magazine of your choice, describing 'My most embarrassing moment'.
> *(16 marks)*

....

....

....

Putting it into practice

Answer the exam-style question below, focusing in particular on sentence variety.

5 You have been asked to write an article for your local paper. Your article will appear as part of a series called 'Making a difference'. Write your article, describing a time when you influenced someone's actions or changed someone's mind, and explaining why and how you did it.

(16 marks)

When you tackle any writing question in the exam, remember to:

- use a range of sentence types
- begin your sentences in a range of different ways
- structure your sentences for effect.

Remember: You will have more space than this to answer the question in the exam. Use your own paper to finish your answer to the question above.

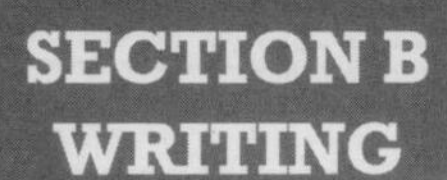

Had a go ☐ Nearly there ☐ Nailed it! ☐

Full stops, question marks and exclamation marks

1 When should you use a full stop? ....

2 When should you use a question mark? ....

3 When should you use an exclamation mark? ....

4 Look at the sentences below. Tick the two sentences that are punctuated correctly. Cross the one that is not.

A I knew that what she had done was wrong, I had to persuade her to do something about it.

B I knew that what she had done was wrong. I had to persuade her to do something about it.

C I knew that what she had done was wrong and I had to persuade her to do something about it.

Now write a sentence explaining your decision. ....

....

....

5 Look at this student's writing. Correct all the full stop, question mark and exclamation mark errors you can find.

A Change of Heart!!

I braced myself for a confrontation, she was looking at me like she knew I had something to say and she didn't want to hear it. My heart began to race and a strange throbbing pain pulsed in my forehead. How could I say it. How could I tell her what I was thinking without upsetting her.

She knew something was coming, tears were welling up in her dark brown eyes and her bottom lip was starting to quiver. I didn't feel much better than she did, my stomach was churning and I could feel my legs shaking. I tried to speak, my mouth felt like sandpaper, it was dry and rough and I couldn't form the words.

You do not use a comma to join two pieces of information in a sentence. Use a full stop to separate them, or a connective to join them. So check every time you use a comma: should it be a comma or a full stop?

Commas

1 Look at the sentences below. Some have used commas correctly. Some have not. Tick the correct sentences and cross the incorrect ones.

Commas in lists

☐ **A** They can comfort us in a crisis, help out when we're in trouble make us laugh or make us cry.

☐ **B** It doesn't matter whether they're tall, short, thin, fat, heart-stoppingly attractive or mirror-crackingly ugly.

☐ **C** She was loud, angry, obnoxious and painfully honest.

Commas in complex sentences with subordinating clauses

☐ **D** Whether we like it or not, friends can hurt as well as help us.

☐ **E** Friends can hurt as well as help us whether we like it or not.

☐ **F** Although I had known her since primary school we never spoke again.

Commas in complex sentences with relative clauses

☐ **G** The problem which we may not want to face, is that friends can sometimes let us down.

☐ **H** A friend who I will not name once told me all my worst faults.

☐ **I** Her house, which I only ever visited once, was enormous.

2 Look again at all the sentences in Question 1. Correct any that you marked as incorrect.

3 Now write **three to five** sentences in response to the exam-style question below, using commas correctly to separate:

- items in a list
- a main and subordinating clause
- a main and relative clause.

> **5** You have been asked to write an article for your school or college website entitled 'The Perfect Friend'. Write your article, describing what you think makes the perfect friend and explaining why. *(16 marks)*

....

....

....

....

....

....

....

....

....

....

....

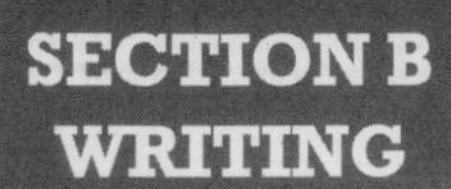

Apostrophes and speech punctuation

1 Look at the sentences below. Some have used apostrophes correctly. Some have not. Tick the correct sentences and cross the incorrect ones.

Apostrophes in contractions

☐ **A** I do'nt see her very often.

☐ **B** I can't believe how things turned out.

☐ **C** She wouldnt answer the phone.

Apostrophes of possession

☐ **D** My teachers' face was a picture.

☐ **E** The school's reaction was incredible.

☐ **F** The boys' faces all lit up.

Speech punctuation

☐ **G** 'I don't believe it!' she shouted.

☐ **H** 'Never mind.'

☐ **I** 'Come over here.' he whispered.

2 Look again at all the sentences in Question 1. Correct any that you marked as incorrect.

Guided **3** Now write a conversation between two friends in which they discuss a boy whose behaviour has resulted in a several teachers ringing his parents. Aim to use apostrophes and speech marks correctly.

'Hey,' she called. 'Come over here.'

'What do you want?' I asked. ....

....

....

....

....

....

....

....

....

Remember:

- apostrophes in contractions are used to replace **missing letters**
- apostrophes of possession are always placed **at the end of the noun** whether it's plural (teachers') or singular (teacher's)
- in dialogue, there is always a punctuation mark **before** the closing speech marks.

Colons, semi-colons, dashes, brackets and ellipses

Colons and semi-colons

1 Look at the sentences below. How could you alter or add to the punctuation, using a colon or a semi-colon?

- **A** There is only one thing you can do to improve your grades. Revise.
- **B** Teachers can help. They can give revision tips and answer any questions you have about the exam.
- **C** Revision isn't easy. It takes time and willpower.
- **D** Exams are the problem. Revision is the solution.

You can use a semi-colon to link two connected ideas instead of using a connective. You can use a colon to introduce:
- a list
- an example
- an explanation.

Dashes and brackets

2 Look at the sentences below. Some have used dashes and brackets correctly. Some have not. Tick the correct sentences and cross the incorrect ones.

☐ **A** My revision – which mainly involves staring into space – began this morning.

☐ **B** A short break (or sometimes a long break) helps clear your mind and recharge your battery.

☐ **C** My bedroom walls are covered in scribbled revision notes and key points (not a pretty sight.

☐ **D** Sometimes I wonder why I bother – and then I remember.

3 Look again at all the sentences in Question 3. Correct any that you marked as incorrect.

4 Now write **three to five** sentences in response to the exam-style question below.

Try to use:
- a colon and a semi-colon
- dashes, brackets and an ellipsis

> 5 You have been asked to write an article for your school or college website entitled 'Revising for beginners'. Write your article, describing your experience of GCSE revision. *(16 marks)*

....

....

....

....

....

....

....

....

....

Putting it into practice

Answer the exam-style question below, focusing in particular on punctuation.

5 A national newspaper is inviting entries for a writing competition. The topic is 'I'll never forget when …' Write your entry, describing an unforgettable experience and explaining what made it so unforgettable. *(16 marks)*

When you tackle any writing question in the exam, remember to:

- use a range of punctuation, including advanced punctuation such as colons and semi-colons
- save time after you have finished writing to check the accuracy of your punctuation.

Remember: You will have more space than this to answer the question in the exam. Use your own paper to finish your answer to the question above.

Common spelling errors 1

Some of the most common spelling errors in students' writing are a result of misusing or confusing:

- would of and would have
- should of and should have
- could of and could have
- our and, are
- their, there, and they're
- affect and effect
- words ending in ley and ely
- its and, it's

1 Identify and correct any spelling errors in these sentences.

A They went all the way back to there house.

B It would of been absolutley unbelievable – if I hadn't seen it with my own eyes.

C One affect of this issue is extremley concerning.

D Their first problem was how to get the students interested.

E Their our three reasons for this.

F There refusing to do anything about it.

G The school offered it's help immediately.

H We felt that students should definitley of been involved.

I Its not only the teachers who our effected by this situation.

J We were forced to reconsider are plan.

K It could not of been achieved without there help.

L Many students felt it had affected them negativley.

M Its not the first time this has happened.

- There are very few words ending in **ley**.
- **Would of**, **could of** and **should of** are **always** incorrect.

Had a go ☐ Nearly there ☐ Nailed it! ☐

Common spelling errors 2

Some of the most common spelling errors in students' writing are a result of misusing confusing:

your and you're

two, too and to

we're, were, where and wear

of and off

whose and who's

passed and past

1 Identify and correct any spelling errors in these sentences:

A He did not know were he was going or who's idea it was.

B To many people make the same mistake.

C The time for worrying has past.

D This has taken some of the pressure of us.

E Your never sure whether you're doing enough to help.

F Whose going to complain about that?

G We where the first people there but still they ignored us.

H They walked passed us as though we wear invisible.

I They went too far, taking it too an extreme.

J How can we tell who's to blame?

K It can be difficult to know when your in the wrong.

L Support for the idea soon began to fall of.

M We simply don't know whose argument to believe and whether were expected to agree or not.

Remember:
A lot is two words. '**Alot** of people make this mistake' is wrong, but '**A lot** of people make this mistake' is correct.

Common spelling errors 3

1 Look carefully at the words below. In each row, one is spelt correctly and the others are spelt incorrectly. Tick the correct spelling, and cross the incorrect spelling or spellings.

argument	arguement	argumant
dificult	difficult	diffacult
disappoint	dissappoint	disapoint
disappear	dissappear	disapear
embarrassing	embarassing	embarasing
possession	possession	posession
beggining	begining	beginning
recomend	recommend	reccomend
occassionaly	ocasionally	occasionally
definately	definitely	definitley
separately	seperately	seperatley
conscious	conshus	concsous
conshence	conscience	concsience
experiance	experance	experience
indapendance	independence	independance
beleive	believe	beleve
weird	wierd	weerd
business	busness	buisness
rythm	rhytm	rhythm
decision	desicion	desision
greatfull	grateful	greatful

2 Now check your answers on page 116. Use the space below to learn and practise any spellings you are not sure about.

Had a go ☐ Nearly there ☐ Nailed it! ☐

Proofreading

1 Look at the extract from one student's writing below. Read it carefully, looking for any:

- spelling errors
- punctuation errors
- grammatical errors – e.g. misused, repeated or missing words.

Circle and correct all the errors you can find.

> Scotland is the most amazing place Ive ever visited, even though it took ten hours to drive there it was worth it the moment i saw were we were staying. Huge blue lochs, rolling green hills, miles and miles of pine forest. They even looked beautiful driving passed them in a a car.
>
> On the first day we took the dogs for a long walk through a forest, it was the quitest place Ive ever been. Even with my brother their, all you could hear was the sound of leafs rustling in the breeze, the birds singing and you're heart beating.
>
> Are hotel was great, the scottish people are so frendly. I would definitley stay there again.

2 Look back at three or four pieces of writing you have completed recently. How many errors can you find? In the table below, note down words which you have misspelled and the **kinds** of punctuation and grammatical errors you have made.

Spelling errors	Punctuation errors	Grammatical errors

Train your proofreading brain to look out for the kinds of punctuation and grammatical errors you are prone to making. When the alarm rings, **stop!** Double check and correct any mistakes.

3 Use the space below to practise and learn all the spellings you have noted in the table.

Putting it into practice

Answer the exam-style question below, focusing in particular on proofreading your answer.

6 'Far too much pressure is placed on young people –pressure from adults, from school and from the media.' Write an article for your school or college website, arguing **either** *for* **or** *against* this view. *(24 marks)*

When you tackle any writing question in the exam, remember to:
- save time after you have finished writing to check the accuracy of your writing
- look out for the spelling, punctuation and grammatical errors which you know you often make.

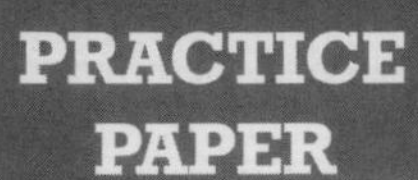

Practice exam paper

This Practice Exam Paper has been written to help you practise what you have learned and may not be representative of a real exam paper.

You will be given more space than this in the exam, so complete your answers on extra paper.

Sources 1, 2 and 3 are provided at the back of this paper.

English/English Language

Unit 1 Understanding and producing non-fiction texts

Time allowed

- 2 hours and 15 minutes

Section A: Reading

Answer **all** questions in this section.

You are advised to spend about one hour on this section.

Read **Source 1**, the newspaper article *Felix Baumgartner: 'I hope I can make fear cool'* by Donald McRae.

1 What do you learn from the article about Felix Baumgartner? *(8 marks)*

8

Now read **Source 2**, the article and the picture which goes with it called, *It's time for pedestrians to reclaim our streets with 20mph speed limit*, by Natalie Bennett and Caroline Lucas.

2 Explain how the headline, sub-headline and picture are effective and how they link with the text. *(8 marks)*

8

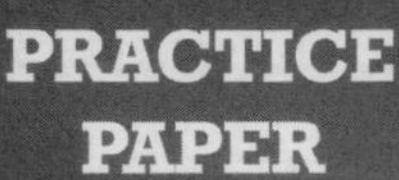

Now read **Source 3**, *Life and Limb*, which is an extract from a non-fiction book.

3 Explain some of the thoughts and feelings Jamie Andrew has as he climbs in the Alps. *(8 marks)*

8

Now you need to refer to **Source 3**, *Life and Limb*, and **either Source 1 or Source 2**.

4 You are going to compare **two** texts, one of which you have chosen.

Compare the ways in which language is used for effect in the two texts.

Give some examples and analyse what the effects are. *(16 marks)*

Turn over ▸

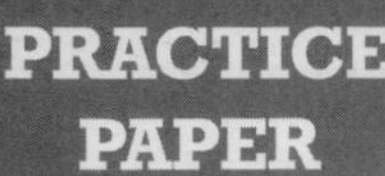

Section B: Writing

Answer **both** questions in this section.

You are advised to spend about one hour on this section.

You are advised to spend about 25 minutes on Question 5.

You are advised to spend about 35 minutes on Question 6.

---

5 A website is inviting entries for a writing competition. The title is 'My Greatest Challenge'.

Write your entry, describing a time when you faced a challenge and explaining how you overcame it.

You should aim to write no more than two and a half sides in response to this question. *(16 marks)*

Turn over ▸

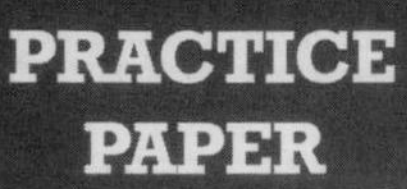

6 'We spend far too much time worrying about how we look. There are much more important things we should be concerned about.'

Write an article for a newspaper, arguing **either** *for* **or** *against* this view. *(24 marks)*

Turn over ▸

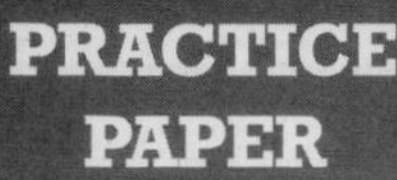

24

Source 1

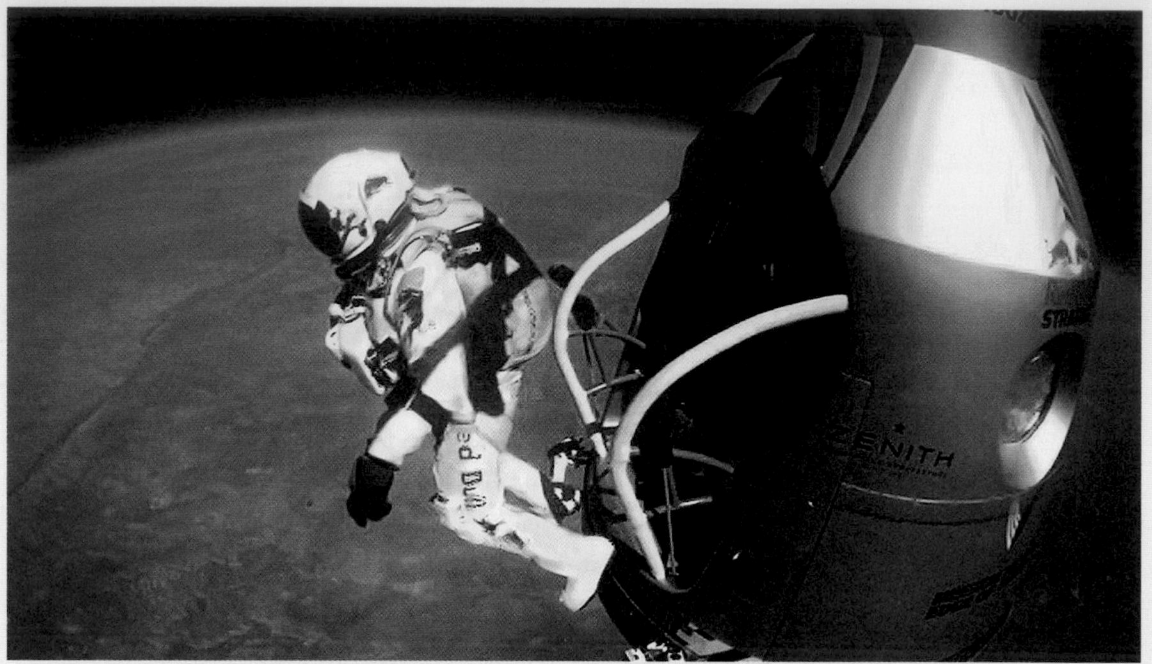

Felix Baumgartner: 'I hope I can make fear cool'

Donald McRae

'They call me Fearless Felix,' says the man who, with nonchalant courage, fell to earth faster than the speed of sound. Less than three weeks ago, Felix Baumgartner reached an altitude of 128,100 feet in a small capsule attached to a helium balloon before he plummeted back down again through 24 miles of cold blackness at a top speed of 833.9 miles per hour.

His space jump was watched live on YouTube by more than eight million people, and the fevered reaction online was matched by saturation coverage in the traditional media. As a curiously driven man, who had dreamed of flying ever since he was a five-year-old boy in Austria, drawing detailed pictures of himself soaring through the sky, Baumgartner had achieved his greatest ambition. He had moved from the often-illegal activity of base-jumping – having blagged his way past lax security at some of the world tallest buildings so his daredevil talents could be noticed – and become one of the world's most celebrated men.

Baumgartner sits in a plush chair in a London hotel and arches a wry eyebrow at his cartoonish nickname. 'You and I know Fearless Felix doesn't really exist,' he says, quietly, and more thoughtfully than might be expected. 'He might seem like a cool guy, but I've had to address a real psychological battle. It's been way harder than stepping out into space.'

He may be a certified celebrity, with an American twang to his Austrian accent, but he talks with the zeal of an ordinary man who has just survived an extraordinary experience. A canny publicist, the 43-year-old is smart enough to recognise that there is real strength in admitting moments of weakness. But there is also something surprisingly moving in his revelations that the source of his suffocating fear was an old-fashioned spacesuit.

'I feared and hated the suit because of my desire for freedom. I started skydiving because I loved the idea of freedom. But you get trapped in a spacesuit, and people are adding weights to it every day.

'I only started getting anxious if I was in the suit more than an hour. You can fight your way through an hour. But if it takes five hours you're never going to win that battle. So that's why I had to address it.'

And so how will a man consumed by outrageous challenges rekindle the intensity of his space jump? 'I don't have to,' he replies, confirming his plan to become a rescue-helicopter pilot. 'I reached a peak and I don't have to top it again. A lot of kids now think of me as Fearless Felix – but I hope I can make fear cool. All these kids can know that Felix also has fear. So they can address their own fears. I did it – at first I would consider the suit a handicap. And handicapped people have to find a way to live with their handicap. The suit was my worst enemy, but it became my friend – because the higher you go, the more you need the suit. It gives you the only way to survive. I learned to love the suit up there. That's an even bigger message than flying supersonic.'

Source 2

It's time for pedestrians to reclaim our streets with 20mph speed limit

Safe, pleasant roads designed for people and communities – not cars – should be the norm where we live, work and shop

Can we make 20mph the default in built-up areas? Photograph: Stephen Kelly/PA

Natalie Bennett and Caroline Lucas

Do you live on a major road? Or a side street in a leafy suburb? Either way, in most parts of Britain, that means you still have vehicles, cars and lorries rushing past your door at 30mph. If, in a moment's inattention you should step out in front of one, it will likely kill you.

Actually, if you are an adult, and reasonably young, you're not so much at risk. Statistics show that it is the young and the old who are most in danger – and poorer people, who are more likely to be walking and more likely to live on busier roads. In Britain 24 per cent of our road deaths are pedestrians – one of the highest percentages in Europe.

The safety argument to reduce speed limits in places where people and cars interact is clear – if you need convincing, you can listen to the emergency services and their experiences, particularly in having to treat child victims. But the benefits of 20mph limits go far beyond that.

It is no coincidence that Britain is the most car-dependent nation in Europe, and the state with the biggest obesity problem. We need to greatly increase 'active transport'– walking and cycling – for the good of our health and wellbeing, as well as to reduce carbon emissions.

We need to ensure that older people feel comfortable crossing the road, secure that cars will have time to see them, and that pedestrian lights allow them enough time to cross. That's the only way they can feel fully able to participate in their communities – with all of the benefits to health and wellbeing that brings.

Make 20mph the default in built-up areas, and we'd get streets all around the country on which the young, the old, all of us could feel much safer, streets we were more inclined to use as pedestrians and as cyclists, pavements that felt more comfortable as a place to stop to catch up with our neighbours. We'd have started to reclaim our streets.

Source 3

Climbing in the Alps, Jamie Andrew remembers the climbing accident that resulted in the amputation of both his arms and legs.

Life and limb

The snow slope sweeps up ahead of us, gently at first, then more steeply where it passes between rocky outcrops. Above, our route joins the crest of the ridge and disappears from view, hidden by the projecting rocks.

The climbing soon becomes more intricate and I have to use my axe to pull myself up over short bulges and steep sections of ice. On the crest of the ridge we weave round massive perched blocks of granite. The drop on either side is breathtaking.

Eventually we come to a wide, level section of ridge, and take the opportunity to have a rest and a bite to eat. I swing my rucksack off my back, push it into the snow and sit down on it. This is a good chance to dry off my legs. The sweat is getting quite uncomfortable.

'Manu,' I ask, 'could you give me a hand, please?'

Manu unzips the lower part of my overtrousers and pushes them back to reveal the carbon fibre and titanium of my artificial legs. With a click of the release button the left leg comes free and Manu pulls it off and plants it beside me in the snow. He does the same with the right leg. The relief is enormous and I stretch out and enjoy the feeling of cool air circulating round my hot stumps.

In the two and a half years since I became a quadruple amputee I have come to accept that I can't do everything for myself all the time. I'm just thankful for all the things I can still do. Constantly being indebted to people isn't such a bad thing either. It brings you closer, builds bonds.

I look up and my gaze travels across the distant mountain, rows of pointed white peaks, like teeth, lining the horizon. Instinctively my eyes find my mountain, Les Droites. I scan its serrated summit ridge.

In a flash I am back there, clinging to that tiny ledge hewn from ice, hard as granite, the Siberian wind rifling through, piercing the many layers of clothing to my very heart. Jamie is beside me, battling with the driving snow that falls in blankets, digging with all his might. And Julio is there too, forcing hot tea between my cracked lips, cutting my rope with his sharp knife, signalling to the helicopter which pitches and rolls like a small boat in high seas. Then my eyes trace out the thin ribbon of ice that marks the decent route, a relatively easy decent, down to the glacier below. The descent we never made.

I will always be there, stranded, with the ice and the wind and the snow. With Julio. With Jamie, the other Jamie – Jamie Fisher – who is gone now forever.

How did this happen to me? Why? What strange twists of fate have taken me from being the bold, independent, carefree climber I was then to become the bizarre individual I am now, without hands, without feet, intent on proving to myself and to the world that I can go on as before? Could things have turned out any different? Questions I have asked myself a thousand times, ask myself a thousand times a day. Now, back in the mountains that so nearly cost me my life, I am searching for answers.

On a day like this it's hard to imagine those desperate scenes of two and a half years ago. Manu laughs as he helps me put my legs back on. I stand up, wobble slightly as my stumps settle into the prosthetic legs, and we climb on.

Answers

SECTION A : READING

1. Questions 1 and 2

1 **(a)** 2
(b) b

2. Questions 3 and 4

1 **(a)** 3a
(b) 4b

3. Planning your exam time

1 15 minutes
2 12 minutes
3 12 minutes
4 12 minutes
5 24 minutes
6 All of them.

4. Reading the questions

1 **(a)** Source 3
(b) Explain
(c) The writer's thoughts and feelings
(d) 8
(e) 12 minutes

2 **Q1:** Source 1; what do you learn; the issues and concerns; 8; 12 minutes
Q2: Source 2; explain how effective and link to text; headline, subheading and picture; 8; 12 minutes
Q4: Source 3 and either Source 1 or 2; compare; language; 16; 24 minutes

5. Approaching the exam paper

1 **Q1:** Source 1; what do you learn; pleasures and pitfalls home improvement; 8 marks.
Q2: Source 2; explain how effective and link to text; headline and picture; 8 marks
Q3: Source 3; explain; thoughts and feelings; 8 marks
Q4: Source 3 and either Source 1 or 2; compare different ways used for effect; language; 16 marks.

2 15 minutes: read questions; skim read source texts; read source texts carefully; read questions and texts again, and highlight relevant information
12 mins: answer Q1
12 mins: answer Q2
12 mins: answer Q3
24 mins: answer Q4

6. Skimming for the main idea

1 World food shortages mean we may have to stop eating meat.
2 Vegetarian food is delicious so we should not worry if world food shortages mean we have to give up eating meat.

7. Annotating the sources

1 B, C and D suggest a strong bond between parent and teenager, the helplessness of the parent, and the pain that this can cause. A and E refer to the teenager more than the parent and so are not relevant to this question.

2 (From Source 1, continuation)

> So what do you do? **Panic**, start refusing to allow your teenager to be 'unknowable'? Start **invading their privacy**, prying into their Internet activity, clipping every wing you can think of? This is the impulse, **the dark side of parental protectiveness**. But perhaps **to succumb to it would be detrimental to everybody**.
> Of course I'm not suggesting turning a blind eye. Even the most unknowable, seemingly adult of teenagers, are still **essentially (not to mention legally) children**. And most are **achingly vulnerable and impressionable** with it. Nor is there any way of sitting back and watching your own child jump into the fire to see what it feels like to get badly burned. Perhaps the trick is to take a breath and understand that in the vast majority of cases **the unknowable child is probably on the right track**. And understand that it might serve us well to stop panicking and try to grasp that, as well as being terrifying, it may be a positive thing. An **essential healthy separation**. A sign that your child is ready to embrace notions of independence and autonomy. To a place – mentally and emotionally – where they need to be. And, yes, dear **panicking, over-protective parents**, that does mean **without you**.
> It's true that older children have a tendency to become secretive, mysterious, sometimes even downright underhand. They **make really stupid decisions and mistakes** – complete howlers. That's why determined, smart parents know they must learn to process this period of child-rearing almost like rolling news, constantly **re-adjusting and updating fact and emotions**. Then if they're lucky and they keep their nerve, they might just get to see **their child walk safely back out of the fog**.

8. Selecting information

1 All of these could be relevant: they suggest an uncomfortable flight on a small and very old aircraft in a remote location.
2 (Source 1, continuation)

> 'Clear prop!' The engine splutters into life. Soon we are cantering along, gathering speed and generously throwing up dust for all and sundry. But there is no all, and there is no sundry, just our guide sitting nonchalantly astride the bonnet of his 4×4 to wave off another batch of **wilderness seekers**. Some distance behind him, **two fire buckets hang, lifeless, from a T-shaped frame next to the lavatory, which has a pointed roof made from sticks. That's it. There is no control tower, no emergency services – just miles and miles of nothingness.**
> We are heading to our camp, **a comfortable oasis of calm** beside the river. By air it is a relatively straightforward journey; back in the 4×4, it would involve a huge amount of **bumping, churning and sliding** over **desert rock and sand** to get there.
> The altimeter needle continues to turn as the views widen; detail is lost as patterns emerge, **nature's patterns**, completely **devoid of influence from man's busying hand**. At cruising height, the desert gives way to mountains, carved and fissured rock massifs.
> **Dry rivers trace steep-sided valleys**, where twin lines of hardy bushes mark the boundaries of an **infrequent flow of water**. But within this seeming barrenness is **life**.
> We have witnessed the **regal oryx** with his lethal horns, striding the plains and scampering up mountain slopes; the **desert-adapted rhino** with his grumpy ways, his lumbering, trundling gait. The list goes on; life goes on, resilient, changing. Then the pilot smiles and offers us a spherical bag. 'We're landing soon to refuel – **anyone for biltong?**'

9. Purpose and audience

1 Purpose: inform
Audience: adults/older teenagers
2 Purpose: persuade
Audience: teenagers/children

3 Purpose: describe
Audience: adults

10/11. Putting it into practice

Example

The article emphasises that climate change is not something we should worry about in a 'distant future'. It is already happening. We are all aware that our weather is becoming more extreme so that 'Heatwaves, floods, droughts and wildfires' are occurring more often. The article points out that this is a symptom of climate change and that scientists have been warning us about this for decades.

The article also points out that scientists are now more able to prove the connection between our weather and climate change. It gives the example that warm weather in November 2010 was made '60 times more likely' due to global warming.

There are some significant consequences of climate change. Some areas are suffering water shortages, others are flooded. Crop harvests are suffering, in particular the US which is facing its worst ever loss.

Finally, the article makes the point that climate change should not be forgotten because of the economic crisis. They should be tackled together.

12. The writer's viewpoint

1 People show their emotions too readily and won't be able to cope when something really serious happens to them.

13. Fact, opinion and expert evidence

1 **(a)** **A** is a fact
(b) **C** is an opinion
(c) **B** is expert evidence

2 GM crops were intended to resist weeds and pests but it seems they do not.

3 **Fact:** The weight of chemicals used has increased by 183 million kilos since 1996; this statistic supports the overall argument, the huge number surprising and shocking the reader.
Opinion: The findings dramatically undermine the case for adopting GM crops; the word 'dramatically' emphasising the writer's viewpoint and directing the reader's response to the facts.
Expert evidence: 'Professor Charles Benbrook said …'; the professor's opinion further supports the writer's viewpoint, further validating it with his expertise and position as university professor.

14. Inference

1 'numbers are increasing'; 'out of control'
2 In increasingly dangerous threat …
3 Key point to make: The writer undermines and dismisses the media hysteria.

15. Point-Evidence-Explain

1 **Evidence A** is more effective because it allows for comment on the writer's language choice.
Evidence B simply repeats the point that children react differently but would not support further explanation.

2/3 **Explain B** is more effective as it focuses more closely on the type of language used and its effect on the reader.

16/17. Putting it into practice

Key points: Ranulph Fiennes is in some ways typical of an older person as he cannot work his phone; but he is adventurous and incredibly tough.

18. Identifying presentational devices 1

Fonts: one bold font for key information; one like a child's handwriting to reflect content
Headings: 'Putting your child first' emphasises hospital's commitment to child health; headings/links on buttons show range of information available
Colour: dominant colours green/white are calm and reassuring, suggesting cleanliness and health; differently coloured link buttons emphasise range of information available
Images: positive images of smiling patients and supportive staff to reassure
Logo: friendly and welcoming logo; plaster represents the care on offer at the hospital

19. Identifying presentational devices 2

Bullet points allow clear and succinct delivery of information.
Tables present a large amount of information clearly and accessibly.
Sections/boxes can be used to highlight key information, separate from the main body of the text.
Paragraphs break information into accessible points.

20. Using P-E-E to comment on presentational devices

1 D, A, F and C, E, B
2 Possible points – e.g. The boy is looking at the book, suggesting the scheme is effective in encouraging him to read.

21. Commenting on headlines

1 A, B, C
2 B
3 C
4 A, D
5 All
6 All

22. Image and effect

1 **A:** might be the most effective choice as it presents school-style food very unattractively.
B: not the most effective choice as it focuses on a smiling canteen worker creating a more positive image of school dinners.
C: not the most effective choice as it focuses on school children, not school dinners.
D: might not be the most effective choice as the article mentions chips but links them to home not school.

23. Linking comments on presentation to the text

1 **Cherish** – an order, directing the reader's response.
Army – suggests a large number of people, well organised.
None of us – includes the reader and writer, creating a shared empathy.
Survive – emphasises, perhaps exaggerates, the importance of these volunteers.

24. Selecting evidence

1/2 **A** Not relevant to the question.
B Suggests her relationship with her father was difficult, emphasised by repetition.
C Suggests her father is tough – both as a cyclist and as a father.
D Emphasises their difficult relationship.
E Suggests she is desperate to win the affection of her emotionally distant father.
Note the extended metaphor that runs throughout the extract: chasing after her father on the bike reflects their emotional relationship.

25. Embedding quotations

1 … parents who 'share a tent at Glastonbury' and 'splash cash'. Worse still, the writer suggests that parents only 'pretend' to be their children's friend, which suggests that their relationship with their children is dishonest.
2 Animals make better parents than humans: they know when it is time to encourage their children's independence.
3 For example: 'the black-headed gull', 'probably a better parent than we humans', 'the young bird adapts', 'The law of our animal kingdom says there's a time to grow up'.
4 Animals such as 'the black-headed gull' can be 'probably a better parent than we humans': they know when it is time to encourage their children's independence because 'The law of our animal kingdom says there's a time to grow up.'

26/27. Putting it into practice

Possible key points:
'global' emphasises scale of the problem
'addiction': dramatic, emotive language
subheading lightens tone with reference to 'manners'
image emphasises anti-social behaviour
'turned off' pun links relationships and phone use.

28. Develop your explanations

1 B, C, D and E are the most relevant and effective comments. A does not fully answer the question.

2 A suggested order would be B, C, E and D.

3 Key points:
emotive language ('shocked and winded') focuses on the physical and emotional effects
use of statistics ('1,000lb beast') emphasises the danger of the situation
'possessed' suggests almost supernatural, emphasising how dangerous and unpredictable the animal is.

29. Word classes

1 For example:
noun – 'handbags'
verb – 'lose'
adjective – 'safe'
adverb – 'exactly'

2 Emphasises the number of times, and the variety of places in which, the writer has lost her handbag.

3 For example: 'diving' suggests the height, steepness and exhilaration of the journey.

4 'blue sky' and 'mountain tops clear' paint the scene vividly but briefly.

30/31. Putting it into practice

Points could include:
problems and frustration emphasised – e.g. repetition of 'I couldn't understand what people were saying; I couldn't speak intelligibly; I couldn't read or write'
'cried' suggests his desperation
'babble' and metaphor of 'my mind wandered round and round in the darkness' vividly describe his struggle
final phrase emphasises his coming to terms with the condition.

32. Connotations

1 **dependency** – connotations of drug addiction, reliance, and quantity
devoured – connotations of quantity but also of choice rather than reliance

2 For example:
slave/master – connotations of control, oppression, supremacy
alien invader – unwanted, unwelcome, threatening.

33. Rhetorical devices 1

1 Alliteration: 'furry friends'
Rhetorical question: 'Why the hell not?'
Repetition: 'Large **ones**, small **ones**. Sucked **ones**, chewed **ones**.'
Lists: 'bears, geese, rabbits …'
Emotive language: 'victims of a firing squad'
Hyperbole: 'victims of a firing squad'
A short sentence: 'Nameless ones.'

34. Rhetorical devices 2

1 For example:
rhetorical question – 'Or are we?'
repetition – '**never** know the love of a human being, **never** sit on a sofa …'
lists – 'never know the love of a human being, never sit on a sofa …'
emotive language – 'enslaved'
contrast – 'picturesque' / 'grotesque'
pattern of three – 'poor rearing, lack of socialisation and lack of health tests'

35. Figurative language

1 'shine' suggests:
intelligence (connotations of brightness)
value (connotations of gold, silver, etc.)

2 'buckets of cold water' suggests:
a shock
extinguishing a fire, suggesting the extinguishing of enthusiasm.

3 'like a plant needs water' suggests that encouragement is essential to life and to growth, and allows children to 'flower' – that is, reach their full potential.

36. Identifying sentence types

1 **A** simple
B complex
C compound
D minor

2 For example:
simple – 'The people of Norwich have an unhappy distinction.'
compound – 'Research suggests that 60 years ago we would spend as much as 18 minutes a day laughing, but that is now down to a paltry 6 minutes.'
complex – 'They laugh just 5.4 times a day on average, which makes them the most sombre souls in the country.'
minor – 'Apparently so.'

37. Commenting on sentence types

1 Short sentences create a sense of tension, suggesting the writer's fear and breathlessness.

2 These still shorter sentences create more tension, suggesting a build up of fear.

3 The writer uses several simple and short compound sentences to heighten the tension still further, suggesting he is building up to a climax.
The use of minor sentences heightens this effect, emphasising the writer's terror and regret at, what he suggests could be, the end of his life.

38/39. Putting it into practice

Key points:
Simile: 'we ate like kings' creates impression of luxurious and tasty meals.
Rhetorical question: 'What, so we could become kitchen slaves, you chauvinist pig?' emphasises the idea that when the author was younger, she felt no need to learn to cook.
List: 'Perhaps they thought we'd be hiring cooks, or our husbands would be doing it, or we'd eat takeaway. Perhaps they assumed we were being taught at home.' shows the alternatives for people who can't cook, demonstrating the need for people to learn.
Contrast: 'It won't be just designing pizza boxes and discussing the importance of washing your hands, but learning to cook a 'repertoire of savoury meals' emphasises that these cookery lessons will be very practical.

40. Making the best comments

1 C1, B2, E3, A4, D5

2 Possible points:
Sentence structure – 'I felt sad and desperately lonely. But I didn't tell anyone.' Two short sentences create blunt and desperate tone.
Language choice – 'best … most glamorous' superlatives build up the writer's expectations.
Viewpoint – irony of the writer and her friend's similar reactions to each other's Facebook pages emphasises the key point that Facebook does not always honestly reflect people's experience.
Effect on reader – rhetorical question on title invites reader to question their own honesty.

41. Comment on language and purpose: argue and persuade

1 The rhetorical question engages the reader, inviting them to consider what they would do in this situation. It implies that no one would do this. The short sentence answers the question firmly and emphatically. The effect of this is to contrast sharply with the expected response to the question, surprising and so further engaging the reader.

2 **(a)** The writer uses emotive language – e.g. 'outraged', 'die' – to emphasise the extreme reactions and emotions which this topic can create.
(b) The writer lists a variety of dangers which pet owners are prepared to face, 'rivers, oceans, fights and fires', to suggest that there is no danger which a pet owner would not face to save the life of their much loved animal.

42. Comment on language and purpose: describe

1 **(a)** **Describing using the five senses:** writer uses a wealth of sensory detail to evoke the scene for the reader – e.g. sight ('a hooded figure'), sound ('of the ocean'), touch ('soft, sandy beach').

Figurative language: compares surfers to praying mantises, comparing them to insects emphasises how small and insignificant they seem in the water; 'praying' suggests an almost religious devotion to their sport.
Language choice: e.g. 'hooded' and 'gliding' suggest a mysterious almost supernatural figure, engaging the reader as we try to work out who he is and what he is doing.
The writer's feelings: does not feature in this extract.

43. Comment on language and purpose: inform and explain

1 The tone of the article is light-hearted and flippant. This is created through informal language – e.g. 'stroppy' – and directly addressing the reader – e.g. 'your'.
2 The tone of the article becomes much more formal as it introduces the scientific study – e.g. 'beneficial', 'important social activities'. This suggests the information is valid and reliable.
3 **(a)** Statistics are used to support the article's main points – e.g. 'Girls aged between 10 and 12 are the happiest group of children' – reinforcing the validity and reliability of the information.
(b) Connectives are not extensively used to signal the article's structure.

44/45. Putting it into practice

Key points:
Opening short sentence is blunt and shocking: 'My last girlfriend was a loser.'
Minor sentences create informal tone: 'Literally.'
The writer emphasises his girlfriend's habit of losing things with a long list: 'keys, money ...'
Contrast of the writer's attitude and his girlfriend's linked through repetition: 'she saw ... I saw ...'
Contrast of metaphor of 'the river of emotion' and the hyperbolic violence of 'push them out of a window'.
Rhetorical questions engage and involve the reader in his argument: '... isn't it?'
Conclusion repeats but inverts the language of the introduction: 'loser' ... keeper'.

46. Looking closely at language

1 **(a)** Purpose: to persuade; tone: aggressive.
(b) For example:
- use of commands – 'bake', 'write', 'give' – is intended to persuade the reader to change their present-buying habits
- 'for God's sake' suggests the writer's frustration.

2 **(a/b)** For example:
- contrast (and connection) of 'gift' and 'junk' in the headline to engage the reader's attention
- repetition/pattern of three – 'nothing they need, nothing they don't own already, nothing they even want' highlights the fact that most gifts are unnecessary
- list – 'electronic drum-machine T-shirt; a Darth Vader talking piggy bank; an ear-shaped iPhone case; a sonic screwdriver remote control ...' emphasises the range and pointlessness of many gifts
- statistics – 'only 1 per cent remain' used as evidence to support the argument
- direct address engages the reader in the argument, encouraging them to question and change their attitude.

3 For example: Final paragraph consists of a long sentence featuring a list of positive alternative 'gifts', sharply contrasted with an emphatic short sentence emphasising their negative environmental impact.

47. Planning to compare language

1 Plans to include key language features, points, evidence and explanation.

48. Comparing language

1 **(a)** describe
(b) persuade

2/3 For example:
Source 1: 'emerald green rainforest dipping leafy fingers' – rich, vivid descriptive language including personification, creates strong visual image for the reader.
Source 2: 'If you're an adventure seeker looking for your next destination to conquer ...' – direct address engages the reader; 'adventure' and 'conquer' suggest challenge and excitement to tempt the reader.

49. Answering a compare question

1 Answers should
- compare the language in the two texts
- focus on the effect of the writer's language choices
- support key point with evidence and explanation/analysis.

50/51. Putting it into practice

Key points
Source 1:
repetition – 'lies, damned lies'
contrast – 'stretching the truth ... lying'
statistic – '5% of undergraduates ...'
emotive language – 'ghastly ... excesses'
rhetorical question – 'Are they kidding?'
complex sentence with very short main clause – 'Looking them straight in the eye with as much wry disbelief as you can muster, smile' contrasts with other possible strategies listed, 'catch teens out in their lies, force confessions out of them, lecture them or get angry'.
Source 2:
rhetorical question – 'What's it really like to be a teenager?'
informal language – 'like when I'm 40-odd'
short informal sentences suggest conversational tone
long complex sentence reflects mum and the relationship relaxing – 'Slowly she's started to trust me more and more, and now she's really relaxed and I'll text her because I respect her.'
final short sentences emphasises change in writer's attitude.

SECTION B : WRITING

52. Reading the questions

1 **(a)** national newspaper
(b) adults, school/college students
2 describe; explain
3 article
4 a school day you particularly enjoyed
5 **(a)** headteacher
(b) arguing
(c) letter
(d) All students should complete at least one month's paid work experience before they leave school / for or against

53. The questions and planning your exam time

1 25 minutes
2 35 minutes
3 **Q5:** 5 mins to plan; 15–17 mins to write; 3–5 mins to check.
Q6: 5 mins to plan; 25–27 mins to write; 3–5 mins to check.

54. Writing for an audience

1 The audience for A is likely to include students, teachers, school governors, and parents. The audience for B is likely to be adults and teenagers.
2 **(b)** The more formal language is more appropriate for a school or college website.
3 **(a)** The more formal opening sentences is more appropriate for the newspaper competition.

55. Writing for a purpose: inform and explain

Answers will vary but students may use subheadings and should use facts or statistics. The tone of the writing should be formal.

56. Writing for a purpose: describe

4 To include examples of:
- the five senses
- figurative language
- physical description of emotion

5 There should be some evidence of conscious redrafting of the response to Question 4.

57. Writing for purpose: argue and persuade

1 Examples of points **for** the point of view could include: 'People spend hours on the Internet';' Like other addictive drugs, people's use increases the more they use it, becoming more and more dependent';' People denied access can suffer cravings'. Examples of points **against** the point of view could include: 'The time people spend on the Internet shows how useful it is';'It does not cause physical harm';'Using the Internet is no different to reading a book or meeting friends, except it is onscreen'.

58. Putting it into practice

1 **Q5:** 25 minutes; **Q6:** 35 minutes

2 **Q5:** purpose – inform/explain; form – article; topic – the most important thing you learned at school.
Q6: audience – adults/older teenagers; form – article; topic – men and women can never be equal.

3 **Q5:** e.g. subheadings, facts/statistics, formal language
Q6: e.g. key points, evidence, rhetorical devices, counter-argument

59. Form: letters and emails

1

Your address
Date

Their address

Dear Mr Smith
I am writing regarding your recent letter to parents and students, dated 13 September

and hope you will consider this before making any decision.
Yours sincerely

Your signature
Your name

2 You do not need to include either addresses or the date in a formal email.

60. Form: articles

Answers will vary but students should include in their article a headline, a subheading, an opening paragraph summing up their ideas and a concluding paragraph. They may also include a quotation.

61. Form: information sheets

Answers will vary but students should include in their information sheet a title, subheadings and evidence of use of structural features such as bullet points, a table, etc.

62. Putting it into practice

Key features/points to include are:
form – your address, the head's address, date, salutation and sign off all correctly laid out.
audience – appropriately formal language
purpose – persuasive points, supported with evidence, use of rhetorical devices and a counter-argument
topic – clear focus on the positive OR negative impact of homework.

63. Planning an answer: describe

Plans to include:
- three or four key ideas
- a range of supporting detail e.g. the five senses, the writer's feelings, details to create mood or atmosphere, language for effect.

64. Planning an answer: inform or explain

Plans to include:
- three or four sequenced key points
- a range of supporting ideas and details.

65. Planning an answer: argue or persuade

Plans to include:
- three sequenced key points
- supporting evidence
- a counter argument
- an introduction and conclusion.

66. Beginnings

Make clear the topic/the argument and include one or two of the suggested approaches, e.g. rhetorical question, bold or controversial statement, quotation, fact or statistic, anecdote.

67. Endings

To include two or more of the suggested approaches, e.g. a vivid image, a warning, a happy note, a thought-provoking question, a 'call to action', reference back to the introduction.

68. Putting it into practice

To include:
- at least three sequenced key points
- supporting evidence
- a counter argument
- an introduction and conclusion

69. Paragraphing

1 **Point:** When students choose …
Evidence: I chose my GCSEs …
Explain: Neither of these reasons …

70. Use connectives

1

Adding an idea	Explaining	Illustrating	Emphasising	Comparing	Contrasting
Moreover … *Furthermore …* *In addition …* *Not only…but also*	*because* *therefore* *consequently*	*For example* *For instance* *Such as*	*In particular* *Especially* *Significantly*	*Similarly* *In the same way*	*However* *On the other hand* *…whereas…*

2 **Scrap 1 examples:** *For example …; therefore…*
Scrap 2 examples: *Moreover … Significantly …; … for instance …*
Scrap 3 examples: *However …*

71. Putting it into practice

To feature:
- well structured paragraphs using clear topic sentences supported with developed detail
- a range of connectives.

72. Getting the right tone

1 Teachers, parents, students.
2 Formal.
3 Teenage gamers.
4 Informal, perhaps using some slang.
5 More formal texts would generally use third person, formal, standard English. Less formal texts might use first person, more informal language and some non-standard English.

73. Synonyms

1 Students: *pupils, exam candidates, learners*
Improve: *develop, enhance, extend*
Learning: *achievement, attainment, skills*
Doing: *completing, achieving, carrying out, performing*

2 embarrassed: *humiliated, ashamed, mortified*
upset: *concerned, worried, alarmed*
scream: *yell, shriek, shout*
moment: *occasion, time, situation*
annoyed: *aggravated, agitated, distressed*

74. Choosing vocabulary for effect: describe

1 Beams of sunlight danced on my walls.

2 The original sentence is over-written. It contains far too much description. Selecting vocabulary carefully is far more effective than cramming in as much description as possible.

75. Choosing vocabulary for effect: argue and persuade

1 **B** Examples include:
use too many > *devour, fritter*
not have enough food > *starve*

C Examples include:
filled with > *dominated by, ruled by*
not like > *hate, detest*
cannot do much about it > *are powerless to change it*

2 'roar' suggests a lion – therefore, loudness, anger, aggression, dominance

3 'howl' suggests loudness, though perhaps ineffectual; 'whimper' suggests weakness.

76. Language for effect 1

1 **A** Rhetorical question.
B Rhetorical question
C Contrast, list.
D Contrast.
E Contrast, list, repetition.
F Repetition.

77. Language for effect 2

1 **A** Hyperbole, alliteration.
B Direct address (and a rhetorical question).
C Alliteration, pattern of three.
D Hyperbole.
E Pattern of three.
F Direct address.

78. Language for effect 3

1 **A** Personification.
B Metaphor.
C Simile.
D Simile.
E Metaphor.
F Personification.

79. Putting it into practice

To include a range of language features including:

- language chosen for effect
- figurative language
- language devices, e.g. rhetorical questions, pattern of three, etc.

80. Sentence variety 1

1 **A** Complex: two verbs, two clauses, linked with *because*.
B Minor: no verb.
C Compound: two verbs, two clauses, linked with *but*.
D Simple: one verb.

2 For example: *Professional footballers are possibly the worst 'fakers'. With just one tap from another player they fall over, dive to the ground or occasionally fly. They always start screaming because it shows they are seriously injured. They say it was a foul. They demand a free kick. Ridiculous.*

81. Sentence variety 2

2 To include at least seven sentences, each beginning with one of:

- a pronoun
- an article
- a preposition
- an -ing word (or present participle)
- an adjective
- an adverb
- a connective

82. Sentences for effect

1 The long sentence emphasises the chain of events, and builds tension as the situation worsens. The short sentence brings it to an abrupt end, focusing on the narrator's horror.

2 **A** emphasises 'her' unsympathetic reaction.
B emphasises the long walk home.
C emphasises the lengthy process of cleaning up.

Note that the information the writer wants to emphasise usually comes at the end of the sentence.

83. Putting it into practice

To include:

- a range of sentence types
- sentences beginning in a range of different ways
- sentences structured for effect.

84. Full stops, question marks and exclamation marks

1 At the end of a sentence.

2 At the end of a question.

3 At the end of an exclamation – but use them sparingly and only one at a time.

4 **A** Incorrect. This is a comma splice: two sentences are joined with a comma; they should be separated with a full stop or joined with a connective.
B Correct. The two sentences are separated with a full stop.
C Correct. The two sentences are joined with a connective.

5 There are eight mistakes in total in the original, including the unnecessary exclamation marks at the end of the title:

A Change of Heart**[1]**

*I braced myself for a confrontation.***[2]** *She was looking at me like she knew I had something to say and she didn't want to hear it. My heart began to race and a strange throbbing pain pulsed in my forehead. How could I say it?***[3]** *How could I tell her what I was thinking without upsetting her?***[4]**

*She knew something was coming.***[5]** *Tears were welling up in her dark brown eyes and her bottom lip was starting to quiver. I didn't feel much better than she did.***[6]** *My stomach was churning and I could feel my legs shaking. I tried to speak.***[7]** *My mouth felt like sandpaper.***[8]** *It was dry and rough and I couldn't form the words.*

85. Commas

1/2 **A** Incorrect: They can comfort us in a crisis, help out when we're in trouble,**[comma needed here]**make us laugh or make us cry.
B Correct.
C Correct.
D Correct.
E Correct.
F Incorrect: *Although I had known her since primary school*,**[comma needed here]***we never spoke again.*
G Incorrect: *The problem*,**[comma needed here]***which we may not want to face, is that friends can sometimes let us down.*
H Incorrect: *A friend*,**[comma needed here]***who I will not name*,**[comma needed here]***once told me all my worst faults.*
I Correct.

86. Apostrophes and speech punctuation

1/2 **A** Incorrect: should be *don't*.
B Correct.
C Incorrect: should be *wouldn't*.
D Incorrect: should be *teacher's* because it is singular (one teacher)
E Correct.
F Correct (plural: several boys' faces)
G Correct.
H Correct.
I Incorrect: *'Come over here*,**[comma needed here]**' *he whispered.*

87. Colons, semi-colons, dashes, brackets and ellipsis

1 Here are some examples of altered punctuation.

A There is only one thing you can do to improve your grades:**[colon, followed by lower case r for revise]** revise.
B Teacher's can help:**[colon, followed by lower case t for they]** they can give revision tips and answer any questions you have about the exam.
C Revision isn't easy:**[colon, followed by lower case i for it]** it takes time and willpower.
D Exams are the problem;**[semi-colon, followed by lower case r for revision]** revision is the solution.

2/3 A Correct.
B Correct.
C Incorrect: *My bedroom walls are covered in scribbled revision notes and key points – not a pretty sight*. (Brackets **must** be used in pairs; dashes can be used singly.)
D Correct.

88. Putting it into practice
Feature a range of punctuation used accurately, including advanced punctuation, such as colons and semi-colons.

89 Common spelling errors 1
1 A *their* (not *there*)
B *would have* (not *would of*); *absolutely* (not *absolutley*)
C *effect* (not *affect*); *extremely* (not *extremley*)
D Correct.
E *There are* (not *Their our*)
F *They're* (not *there*)
G *its* (not *it's*)
H *definitely have* (not *definitely of*)
I *It's* (not *Its*); are affected (not *our effected*)
J *our* (not *are*)
K *could not have been* (not *could not of been*); *their* (not *there*)
L *negatively* (not *negativley*)
M *It's* (not *Its*)

90. Common spelling errors 2
1 A *where* (not *were*), *whose* (not *who's*)
B *too* (not *to*)
C *passed* (not *past*)
D *off* [US] (not *of* [US])
E *You're* (not *Your*)
F *Who's* (not *Whose*)
G *were* (not *where*)
H *past* (not *passed*), *were* (not *wear*)
I *to* [an extreme] (not *too*)
J Correct.
K *you're* (not *your*)
L *off* (not *of*)
M *we're* (not *were*)

91. Common spelling errors 3
1 argument
difficult
disappoint
disappear
embarrassing
possession
beginning
recommend
occasionally
definitely
separately
conscious
conscience
experience
independence
believe
weird
business
rhythm
decision
grateful

92. Proofreading
1 The corrections are in **bold**.
Scotland is the most amazing place **I've** ever visite**d. Even** though it took ten hours to drive there it was worth it the moment **I** saw **where** we were staying: huge blue lochs, rolling green hills, miles and miles of pine forest; **they** even looked beautiful driving **past** them in a car.
On the first **day,** we took the dogs for a long walk through a forest. **It** was the quietest place **I've** ever been. Even with my brother **there**, all you could hear was the sound of **leaves** rustling in the breeze, the birds singing and **your** heart beating. **Our** hotel was great**;** the **Scottish** people are so **friendly**. I would **definitely** stay there again.

93. Putting it into practice
Featuring accurately used spelling and punctuation and possibly signs of going back through the answer making corrections.

There are no questions printed on this page.

Published by Pearson Education Limited, Edinburgh Gate, Harlow, Essex, CM20 2JE.

www.pearsonschoolsandfecolleges.co.uk

Text and original illustrations © Pearson Education Limited 2013
Edited, produced and typeset by Wearset Ltd, Boldon, Tyne and Wear
Cover illustration by Miriam Sturdee

First published 2013

17 16 15 14
10 9 8 7 6 5 4

British Library Cataloguing in Publication Data
A catalogue record for this book is available from the British Library

ISBN 978 1 447 94070 8

Printed in Slovakia by Neografia

Acknowledgements
The publisher would like to thank the following for their kind permission to reproduce their photographs:

(Key: b-bottom; c-centre; l-left; r-right; t-top)

Alamy Images: Juice Images 38, Malcolm Park France Images 108, MBI 22 (b), Tetra Images 18l; **Getty Images:** Cultura/Liam Norris 26, Photographer's Choice/David Young-Wolff 20, Stone/Charlie Schuk 22 (a); **Masterfile UK Ltd:** 18c, Monkey Business Images 18r; **Pearson Education Ltd:** Clark Wiseman/Studio 8 22 (c); **Rex Features:** 38, Red Bull Content Pool 104; **Shutterstock.com:** Stephen Rees 106; **Veer/Corbis:** Orange Line Media 50, Roman_Shyshak 22 (d)

All other images © Pearson Education Limited

We are grateful to the following for permission to reproduce copyright material:

Extracts adapted from 'Forget meat – there's a world of vegetarian food out there', *The Guardian*, 28/08/2012 (Lagusta Yearwood); and 'How hard it can be to know your child', *The Observer*, 29/09/2012 (Barbara Ellen), copyright © Guardian News & Media Ltd 2012; Extract from 'Just back: The Skeleton Coast from above', *The Daily Telegraph*, 15/06/2012 (John Roome), copyright © Telegraph Media Group Limited, 2012; Extract from 'Get used to "extreme" weather, it's the new normal', *The Guardian*, 19/09/2012 (Connie Hedegaard), copyright © Guardian News & Media Ltd 2012; Extracts abridged from 'We have become a nation of cry-babies!', *The Daily Mail*, 01/10/2012 (Jan Moir); and 'How GM crops have increased the use of danger pesticides and created superweeds and toxin-resistant insects', *The Daily Mail*, 02/10/2012 (Sean Poulter), copyright © Daily Mail 2012; Extract abridged from 'They are as big as Alsatians and getting bigger', *The Guardian*, 07/06/2012 (Stephen Harris), copyright © Guardian News & Media Ltd 2012; Extracts from 'Coping with the first day at school', *The Daily Telegraph*, 05/09/2012 (Rachel Halliwell); and 'Sir Ranulph Fiennes: it's the winning that is important', *The Daily Telegraph*, 02/10/2012 (Harry Wallop), copyright © Telegraph Media Group Limited, 2012; Extract from 'Top Footballers See Pay Rise By 1500%'. Sky, 20/08/2012, http://news.sky.com, Reproduced with permission; Extract from 'The dogs who listen to children reading', *The Guardian*, 28/02/2011 (Patrick Barkham), copyright © Guardian News & Media Ltd 2011; Extract abridged from 'Cherish the grey army of volunteers – none of us would survive without their dedication', *The Independent*, 01/10/2012 (Natalie Haynes), copyright © The Independent www.independent.co.uk; Extract from *Between the Lines* by Victoria Pendleton, HarperSport, 2012, pp.9–10. Reprinted by permission of HarperCollins Publishers Ltd © 2012 Victoria Pendleton; Extract from 'My message to the parents who can't let their children go: grow up', *The Observer*, 05/08/2012 (Phillip Hodson), copyright © Guardian News & Media Ltd 2012; Extract from 'The new global addiction: smartphones', *The Daily Telegraph*, 15/06/2012 (Damian Thompson), copyright © Telegraph Media Group Limited, 2012; Extract from 'I was crushed by a cow', *The Guardian*, 15/06/2012 (Mike Scriven), copyright © Guardian News & Media Ltd 2012; Extract from 'At a loss in the Rocky Mountains', *The Daily Telegraph*, 05/10/2012 (Linda Fawke), copyright © Telegraph Media Group Limited, 2012; Extract abridged from 'Experience: I lost the power of language', *The Guardian*, 21/09/2012 (Andy McKillop), copyright © Guardian News & Media Ltd 2012; Extract abridged from 'Treat it well and telly will be a faithful family friend', *The Daily Telegraph*, 09/10/2012 (Rowan Pelling), copyright © Telegraph Media Group Limited, 2012; Extracts adapted from 'Time to let the furry friends go', *The Guardian*, 29/09/2012 (Nick Coleman); and 'Battery-farmed puppies are a shame on our nation', *The Guardian*, 21/09/2012 (Beverley Cuddy), copyright © Guardian News & Media Ltd 2012; Extracts from 'A poor school report is no barrier to succes', *The Daily Telegraph*, 10/01/2012 (Max Davidson); and 'No laughing matter', *The Daily Telegraph*, 08/10/2012, copyright © Telegraph Media Group Limited, 2012; Extract abridged from *The Accidental Adventurer* by Ben Fogle, published by Bantam Press, 2012, pp.11–12. Reprinted by permission of The Random House Group Limited and Lucas Alexander Whitley Ltd on behalf of Rambling Ruminations Ltd; Extracts abridged from 'How I learned to cook?', *The Guardian*, 23/02/2013 (Esther Walker); 'Is your Facebook page a lie?', *The Guardian*, 08/10/2012 (Libby Page); and 'I'd risk my life to rescue my dog; that's just what owners do', *The Guardian*, 28/09/2012 (Michele Hanson), copyright © Guardian News & Media Ltd 2012, 2013; Extract abridged from 'Just back: from dawn to dusk on Bondi Beach', *The Daily Telegraph*, 18/05/2012 (Janet Rogers), copyright © Telegraph Media Group Limited, 2012; Extract from 'Having friends and going swimming are more important than money to today's youth', *The Daily Mail*, 07/10/2012, copyright © Daily Mail 2012; Extracts abridged from 'MY LAST GIRLFRIEND was a loser', *The Guardian*, 15/02/2010 (Jon Richardson); 'Splashes of Beauty', *The Guardian*, 29/01/2009 (Poorna Shetty); 'Ask the experts: painting vacations and adventure sports', *The Guardian*, 17/08/2012; and 'What does being a dad mean?', *The Guardian*, 30/06/2012 (Sarfraz Manzoor and John Crace), copyright © Guardian News & Media Ltd 2009, 2010, 2012; Extract from 'Is it just me?', *The Daily Telegraph*, 24/09/2012 (Miranda Hart), copyright © Telegraph Media Group Limited, 2012; Extract from 'Lies, damned lies, and teenagers', *The Guardian*, 02/07/2009 (Anne Korpf), copyright © Guardian News & Media Ltd 2009; Extract abridged from 'What's it really like to be a teenager?', *The Independent*, 14/07/2012 (Charlotte Phibly), copyright © The Independent www.independent.co.uk; Extracts in Practice Paper from 'Felix Baumgartner: "I hope I can make fear cool"', *The Guardian*, 03/11/2012 (Donald McRae); and 'It's time for pedestrians to reclaim our streets with 20 mph speed limit', *The Guardian*, 01/11/2012 (Natalie Bennett & Caroline Lucas), copyright © Guardian News & Media Ltd 2012; Extract in Practice Paper from *Life and Limb* by Jamie Andrew, A.M. Heath & Co Ltd, 2005, copyright © Jamie Andrew, 2005. Reproduced by permission of A.M. Heath & Co Ltd and Little, Brown Book Group.

Every effort has been made to contact copyright holders of material reproduced in this book. Any omissions will be rectified in subsequent printings if notice is given to the publishers.

In the writing of this book, no AQA examiners authored sections relevant to examination papers for which they have responsibility.